Tales of a city

LONDON

Adventure
Walks

for families

Tales of a city

LONDON

Adventure

Walks

for families

Becky Jones & Clare Lewis

FRANCES LINCOLN LIMITED
PUBLISHERS

This book belongs to

. . . .

Frances Lincoln Limited
4 Torriano Mews
Torriano Avenue
London NW5 2RZ
www.franceslincoln.com

London Adventure Walks for families
Copyright
© Frances Lincoln Limited 2010
Text and drawings copyright
© Becky Jones and Clare Lewis 2010
Maps by Frances Bennett

Drawings by the Martin (Lewis) children,
Edward, Isabella, Ottoline, and the Crichton-
Miller (Jones) children, Alex, Harry and Freddie

ISBN 978-0-7112-3067-5

Printed in China

9 8 7 6 5 4 3 2 1

contents

Travel in London

- **London Transport** is centrally coordinated by Transport for London (TFL); call 020 7222 1234 (24 hours) or go to www.tfl.gov.uk. This includes information on overground and underground trains, buses and boats.
- **Tickets and travel cards** The cheapest and most convenient way to travel around London by public transport is with an Oyster card. These work on buses, London Underground, London Overground, Docklands Light Railway, National Rail within London and various river boats (including the Thames Clipper). Or you can buy a daily travel card. Be aware that in the centre of London you can no longer just hop on a bus and buy a ticket – you have to buy them before you get on from ticket machines at bus stops, which require the right money (cards not accepted). Foreign tourists can buy a special Tourist Oyster card.
- **Children's travel** All children under eleven travel free. Children and young adults aged between eleven and eighteen in full-time education can get a Zip card – a free Oyster photocard. With a Zip card travel is free on all buses and is much reduced on underground and overground trains. If you live in London, you can apply for a Zip card at www.tfl.gov.uk. If you live outside London, you can still apply for a non-residential card at a cost of £5. Expect the process to take three weeks. The card can be collected from a designated central London station. Child fares are available if you don't have a Zip card.
- **Boat services** See the TFL website as there are numerous different private boat companies. The Thames Clipper is the fast(ish) commuter boat; the leisure services boats tend to be slower and more of a cruise. Children under five go free on all boats, but five to eleven year olds must buy a child ticket. Oyster cards are accepted and receive discounts on Thames Clippers and some other boats.
- **National Rail Enquiries** call 08457 48 49 50 or visit www.nationalrail.co.uk.

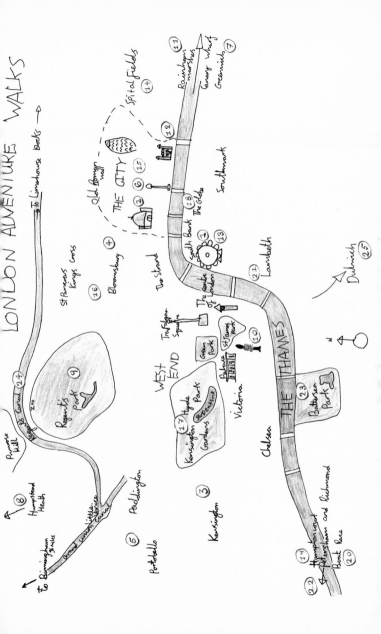

Composed upon Westminster Bridge

The City now doth, like a garment, wear
The beauty of the morning; silent, bare,
Ships, towers, domes, theatres, and temples lie
Open unto the fields, and to the sky

William Wordsworth

Introduction

London Adventure Walks for families is packed with urban adventures with a child-centred twist, to help you and your family explore this great city and get the best out of your visit, whether you are a Londoner or a tourist. Discover the secret places, hidden treasures, world-famous landmarks, remarkable people and dramatic history that make up London's colourful story.

The book includes twenty-five imaginative walks, in the course of which you will unearth what the Romans did for London, eat buns with Paddington Bear, chop off heads with the Tudors, chase Oliver Twist down murky alleyways, visit Shakespeare's Globe, shop in London's hippest markets and have a pirates' duel with Captain Hook. *London Adventure Walks* will guide you to all the must-do places and top sights of London, and you will meet characters and hear stories that will enthuse children and adults alike.

We've tried to squeeze in everything a curious child might like to know who built what; who lived where; what happened when; plus lots of intriguing London facts. We've also thought about the practicalities: how to get there; places to picnic; maps; websites; key museums and galleries; and what to look out for on the way. Whether you live here or not, be a tourist for the day: stuff a copy of *London Adventure Walks* and an *A–Z* in a backpack and have a great day out.

Twenty-five fun things to do before you grow up

1   Climb the Monument for a great view of the City
2   Test out the Whispering Gallery at the top of St Paul's Cathedral
3   See the stars at the Greenwich Planetarium
4   Take the last foot ferry in London across the river
5   Fly a kite from the top of Parliament Hill
6   Run across the Millennium Footbridge
7   March with the soldiers at the Changing of the Guard
8   Eat jellied eels at a London street market
9   Go mudlarking on the Thames foreshore
10   Swim in one of London's open-air pools
11   Ride a horse in Hyde Park alongside the Household Cavalry
12   Go birdwatching on Rainham Marshes
13   See a show at a puppet theatre
14   Take a spin on the London Eye
15   Wave a flag at the Lord Mayor's Show
16   Bicycle along the Regent's Canal
17   Take a space-age ride on the Docklands Light Railway
18   Float in a boat up the Thames
19   Step back in time in a Georgian house in Spitalfields
20   Take part in a London festival
21   Be dazzled by the Crown Jewels
22.   Pick blackberries in an ancient woodland
23   Watch free street theatre at Covent Garden
24   Skateboard under the Festival Hall
25   Cheer on your favourite London team at a football match

Reed warbler

1. Landmark London: the best sights in the shortest time

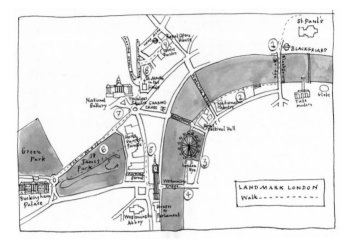

The Adventure

For those of you who have just arrived in London or haven't done the tourist thing for years, we've created a quick taster (or refresher), get your bearings kind of walk that will take you past as many of London's most famous landmarks as possible in a couple of hours.

How far? 4.8 km/3 miles
Start St Paul's tube **Finish** Covent Garden tube

Walk the Walk

1. Come out of the tube by exit 2 and turn left down Panyer Alley. Turn right on St Paul's Churchyard and walk past the Cathedral. Head straight on down Ludgate Hill. Turn left at New Bridge Street and walk straight on to and over Blackfriars Bridge. Ahead of you is the towering chimney of

the Tate Modern art gallery in the old Bankside Power Station. To its left is the reconstruction of Shakespeare's timber-framed Globe theatre.

2. Cross over to Doggett's pub and hop down the stairs towards the river. Head west along the Thames Path, passing the Oxo Tower, the National Theatre, the National Film Theatre and the Festival Hall. There are often street performers and free events along this stretch, as well as skateboarders and bikers, pavement artists and musicians.

3. Pass under Waterloo Bridge, heading for the London Eye, the great wheel where you can ride high over London.

4. When you reach Westminster Bridge, cross back over the river. Big Ben and the Houses of Parliament are on your left.

5. Turn right into Whitehall. Quite soon you'll pass the bottom of Downing Street, where the Prime Minister lives. Peer through the railings and see who you can see: there is always a policeman on the doorstep of No. 10. Walk on until you get to the guards on horseback at the entrance to Horse Guards Parade. Turn left between the guards, crossing over to St James's Park.

6. Run through the park, all the way to the end to see Buckingham Palace. If the flag is up, the Queen is at home.

7. Walk all the way back down the Mall, through Admiralty Arch to Trafalgar Square. Look out for the ships on the

Big Ben

The famous clock tower, designed by Pugin, that we all call Big Ben is more properly called the Great Clock of Westminster. Big Ben is actually one of the bells inside it. Striking on the hour, it weighs 13.8 tonnes and is one of the heaviest bells in England. If you are eleven or over you can ask your MP to arrange a tour.

LONDON SIGHTS

Admiralty Arch

Big Ben

Buckingham Palace

London Eye

National Gallery

Nelson's Column

top of each lamp-post, representing Lord Nelson's fleet, and head for the 52m/170ft high Nelson's Column dominating the centre, the stone lions at each corner, the fountains and the National Gallery. The columns here were taken from one of George IV's old palaces. Trafalgar Square is the very centre of London.

8. Walk across the top of Trafalgar Square towards St Martin-in-the-Fields church. Turn left up St Martin's Place. Take the right fork into St Martin's Lane, passing the London Coliseum, home of the English National Opera.

9. Take a right down the narrow street New Row, and continue straight on down King Street, to the cafés, bars, street entertainers and shops of Covent Garden for something to eat or drink, or just to stop and take in the free entertainment.

Turn left at the centre of the market, towards James Street and Long Acre, to take the tube back from Covent Garden station.

Useful information

The official London Tourist Board website is www.visitlondon.com. Book a ride on the London Eye www.londoneye.com.

A London scavenger hunt

You may need to play this over a long stretch of time. You could have fun building up a scrapbook of London finds.

- A bus ticket
- A pigeon feather
- A plane tree leaf/seed (depending on the time of year)
- A clay pipe from the banks of the Thames
- A photo or sketch of a statue (name one)
- A certificate for climbing the Monument
- A sighting of a parakeet

2. Out of the Ashes: the Great Fire of London

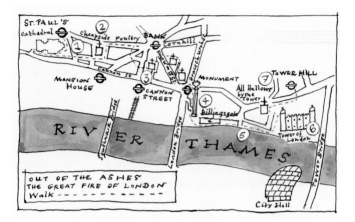

The map shows locations along the River Thames including St. Paul's Cathedral, Cheapside, Poultry, Bank, Cornhill, Cannon St, Mansion House, Cannon Street, Monument, All Hallows by the Tower, Tower Hill, Billingsgate, Southwark Bridge, London Bridge, Tower of London, Tower Bridge, City Hall.

Out of the Ashes / The Great Fire of London / Walk - - - - -

The Adventure

In 1666 the City of London was practically razed to the ground by the Great Fire of London. Starting on Sunday 2 September at Thomas Farriner's bakery on Pudding Lane, at approximately one o'clock in the morning, it raged for four days. The fire spread fast via warehouses and shops full of combustible materials. A strong easterly wind fanned the flames along the narrow streets of timber houses. By 7 a.m., 300 houses had been destroyed. By the time the fire was put out, St Paul's Cathedral, 44 livery halls, 13,200 houses and 87 churches were gone and a hundred thousand people were homeless. Astonishingly, there were only six recorded deaths; but it is impossible to be sure how many people actually died. What is certain is that many people who had survived the Great Plague of 1665 had now lost everything.

It took thirty years to rebuild London and cost £10 million. The new city followed the footprint of the medieval street plan but with improvements: brick houses; wider streets; new pavements and sewers. Sir Christopher Wren was the chief architect of Charles II's vision and his work has shaped the city we see today. Climb the dome of St Paul's Cathedral, the apogee of Wren's work, survey the city streets from the top of the Monument, built to commemorate the Great Fire, and open the door to some of the fifty-one new churches resurrected from the ashes. Bring a picnic to enjoy on the Thames shore, some gloves to mudlark and an appetite for brass rubbing.

How far? 3.2 km/2 miles
Start St Paul's tube **Finish** Tower Hill tube

Walk the Walk

1. Leave St Paul's tube by exit 2 and turn left down Panyer Alley, then right into St Paul's Churchyard. Walk through the courtyard to the steps of the Cathedral. With its European-style dome St Paul's was an extraordinarily radical concept in architecture at the time, and remains a relic of Wren's thwarted dream to redesign London as an Italianate city. The cathedral, which took thirty-five years to build, is 108.4m/355½ft high. The gold ball and cross on top is 7m/23ft high and weighs about 7 tonnes. Walk up the 259 steps of the spiral staircase to the Whispering Gallery and try out its clever acoustic – if you whisper on one side of the gallery it is audible all the way round the other side. Keep going up to the Golden Gallery – making your climb a total of 528 steps – and you will be rewarded with a panorama of the city. At the time of the Fire St Paul's was stuffed with people's belongings. They thought a stone building wouldn't catch fire; but by 8 p.m. on the Tuesday, the third day of the fire, it had succumbed.

2. Turn left out of the Cathedral and round it to New Change. Cross over, turn left and then right into Watling Street, then take a left up Bow Lane to St Mary-Le-Bow. This is one of the 'new' churches designed by Sir Christopher Wren; it is immortalized

in the nursery rhyme 'Oranges and Lemons'. Turn right into Cheapside, and take a distant look at the Guildhall on your left at the top of King Street. This was the only non-ecclesiastical stone building that survived the Great Fire; valuables were hidden in the crypt as the fire leapt up Cheapside. At No. 1 Poultry, built on the site of St Benet Fink church, a casualty on day two of the fire, turn right down Bucklersbury Passage, once the centre of the apothecary business, also destroyed in the blaze.

3. Cross over Queen Victoria Street to look at the church of St Stephen Walbrook, thought to be a practice run for St Paul's, as it also has a dome. This church exemplifies Wren's innovative approach to church architecture: unlike their predecessors Wren's churches are straight-sided rectangular buildings with uncluttered internal spaces. The purposely generous-sized, clear-paned windows meant they were filled with light and the pulpit was placed in the heart of the church with the congregation surrounding it, making it a more inclusive layout. Architecture guru Nicholas Pevsner, who painstakingly charted the buildings of the United Kingdom, lists St Stephen Walbrook as one of the ten most important buildings in England. Leaving the church, turn right down an alley, St Stephen's Row, alongside the church, following the passageway round to the right (don't go down

OPPOSITE THIS SITE STOOD ST.MARGARET FISH STREET HILL DESTROYED IN THE GREAT FIRE 1666

Mansion House Place) and left on to St Swithin's Lane, where Salter's Hall burnt down. Walk straight ahead into King William Street and cross over. Pass St Mary Woolnoth, the only Nicholas Hawksmoor church within the City boundary. Turn right into Lombard Street, which the fire was raging down by 10 o'clock on Monday morning. At St Edmund King and Martyr church turn right down Clement's Lane to look at St Clement Eastcheap, thought to be built by Wren. A record notes 'one third of a hogshead of wine, given to Sir Christopher Wren, £4 2s', assumed to be his design fee. Carry on past the church and turn left on to King William Street. Keep left, cross over Gracechurch Street at the lights, and continue on King William Street.

4. Turn right down Pudding Lane to Wren's Monument to the Great Fire: a 61m/200ft Doric column. Its height is the exact distance between here and the bakery in Pudding Lane where the fire began. Climb the 311 stairs and be rewarded with a certificate and one of the best views in London, especially of the dome of St Paul's. Continue down Fish Street Hill and cross over Lower Thames Street, following the path of the fire, which, as it headed to London Bridge, razed to the ground the church of St Magnus the Martyr. Inside the rebuilt St Magnus, designed by Wren, is a model of London Bridge from the time of the Fire. As you exit the church turn left on to Lower Thames Street. Take the steps on the left, and then turn left again up another

The Monument

The Great Plague of 1665

The plague takes three forms. In *bubonic* plague, disease invades the body's lymphatic system by way of an infected flea-bite, leading to painful swellings called buboes in the glands at the throat, armpits and groin. *Pneumonic* plague occurs when the infection goes straight to the lungs; this form of the disease is spread by sneezing and coughing. Either bubonic or pneumonic plague can lead to the most deadly form of all, *septicaemic* plague, when the disease enters the bloodstream.

In the early 1660s a wave of bubonic plague, carried by the fleas from infected rats, spread slowly westward across Europe. By late 1664 it had reached the port of Yarmouth and by March 1665 it had taken hold in the slums of St-Giles-in-the-Fields, just outside the City walls. The King's court and the wealthy left London. But the poor were condemned to stay where they were. Draconian measures were taken. Victims were shut in their homes; red crosses were painted on the doors and guards kept watch to make sure no one entered or left the premises except for the dreaded plague nurses. Markets were suspended and public meeting places such as pubs were closed. Despite this, the disease spread fast and by late August four thousand people were dying each week. In the week ending 19 September the weekly toll peaked at 7,165 deaths from plague alone. In total 68,575 deaths from plague were recorded in the Bills of Mortality for London but the true figure was probably more than 100,000 – approximately one-third of the population. Most of these people were buried in mass graves outside the city. The Great Fire of the following year did at least bring one benefit, as it stopped the terrible disease in its tracks.

flight to London Bridge: saved from the fire because an earlier fire had burnt down some houses and shops, leaving a fire-break the flames could not leap.

5. Take the steps to the Thames Path heading east. Pass Billingsgate, the fish market made by Act of Parliament a free and open market for 'all sorts of fish whatsoever', with one exception: the sale of eel was restricted to Dutch fishermen, who had helped feed the people of London in the 1666 crisis. Walk on to the Custom House, where duties on cargoes were calculated, a victim of the fire and rebuilt to Wren's design. Just beyond here is a good place to get to the river for a picnic and mudlarking (see page 97). Charles II and his brother the Duke of York came along the river in a royal barge to observe the fire. They took charge of the fire-fighting operations and set up fire posts manned by a hundred civilians and thirty foot soldiers.

6. Keep going along Sugar Quay Walk, past the Tate and Lyle jetty and along Three Quays Walk, approaching the outer

Fire Facts

- People left the city for the high ground of Moorfields, Parliament Hill and Islington.
- The Royal Navy were called in to use gunpowder to blow up houses to create fire-breaks.
- Burn marks from the Great Fire scarred the door of the church of All Hallows by the Tower; they could be seen until the church was bombed in the Blitz of the 1940s.
- Many thought the fire had been started deliberately, and a scapegoat was found: a Frenchman, Robert Hubert, who was tried, and hanged.
- There was no official London fire brigade until 1866: each parish kept buckets, axes, fire hooks and ladders to fight fires.
- There was no insurance so Londoners had to pay for their burnt houses to be rebuilt.

limits of the fire which, at 9 p.m. on Monday 3 September was just 300 yards from the Tower of London. All the remaining fire engines at Woolwich and Deptford Naval Yards were mobilized to stop the fire from engulfing the Tower.

7. At the Tower, walk up the hill and turn left to visit the church of All Hallows by the Tower. It is from this tower that the famous diarist and clerk to the Royal Navy Samuel Pepys looked out over the city in despair as it burned. His diaries are an important source of information about the fire, including personal anecdotes: he buried his wine and Parmesan cheese in his back garden in Cloak Lane to protect them from being lost in the fire. While you are in the church, have a go at brass rubbing and delve into the treasure trove museum in the crypt. Leave the way you came in and walk back towards the

Tower. Don't go to the river, keep going straight and turn left into the underpass to Tower Hill tube station.

Eat me, drink me

Pack for a Thames-side picnic. Otherwise, on weekdays there are plenty of cafés in the City, though they're not always open on weekends. There is a sandwich kiosk at the Tower.

Useful information

- St Paul's Cathedral 020 7246 8357 www.stpauls.co.uk
- The Monument 020 7626 2717 www.themonument.info
- The Tower of London 0844 482 7777 www.hrp.org.uk
- For brass rubbing at All Hallows by the Tower call
  020 7481 2928 or see www.ahbtt.org.uk

Further afield

The Museum of London, London Wall, London EC2Y 5HN, 020 7001 9844, www.museumoflondon.org.uk, has the definitive Great Fire of London exhibition.

Books to read

Two great dramas set against the backdrop of the Great Fire: *Forged in the Fire* by Ann Turnbull; *Raven Boy* by Pippa Goodhart

Did you know?

- During the Great Fire the price of hiring a cart went up from a few shillings to £30 or even more.
- The Old Wine Shades near the Monument is the only City tavern to have survived the Great Fire. The Hoop and Grapes in Aldgate, a house at the time, is the only remaining timber-framed building that survived the Fire.

3. Mission Impossible: Spies and the Cold War

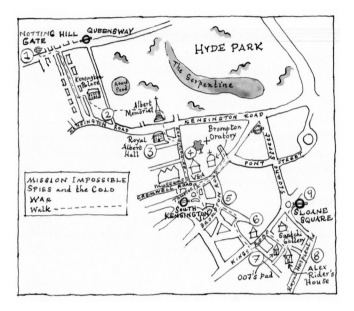

The Adventure

During the Cold War – the period of stand-off between the United States and the Soviet Union and their respective allies that lasted from 1945 until 1989 – a war of spies and spying was played out on the streets of London. Kensington, with its central location, winding streets, public buildings and many foreign embassies, was at the heart of clandestine activity. Find out where the real spies did their dead letter drops, track down the key embassies, see where the famous Cambridge Five spy ring used to meet, and discover where fictional spy heroes James Bond and Alex Rider live. On the way take this opportunity to brush up spy skills, give yourself a code name, learn real secret agent jargon and write your own secret message.

How far? 6.4 km/4 miles
Start Notting Hill Gate tube
Finish Sloane Square tube

Walk the Walk

1. Come out of the tube station on the south side, following the signs for Notting Hill Gate and Kensington Church Street. Turn left and keep going up Notting Hill Gate until you reach the third turning on the right. Walk through the rather grand gates into Kensington Palace Gardens. This half-mile-long tree-lined avenue is one of the most exclusive addresses in London. The large detached houses are in the grounds of Kensington Palace and are part of the Crown Estate – notice the gas street lamps. In your role as secret agent make a note of the embassies and ambassadorial residences: see how many countries you can identify from the flags you see. This street saw wartime action as the location of the 'London Cage', a prisoner of war camp run by MI9, who gleaned information from enemy prisoners during World War II. Walk most of the length of the road but before reaching the end take the turning on the left into Kensington Gardens alongside Kensington Palace, where Queen Victoria was born and lived until she moved into Buckingham Palace on her accession to the throne. The Palace is open to the public and worth a visit.

2. Stride out across the park towards the Round Pond, leaving the front entrance of the Palace behind you. Look out for the spire of the Albert Memorial on the horizon further ahead on the right and make a beeline for it. A memorial to Prince Albert, it celebrates the Prince's passions and Victorian achievements. The figures at the top represent manufacture, commerce, agriculture and engineering. The Parnassus frieze

FLAGS YOU MIGHT SEE

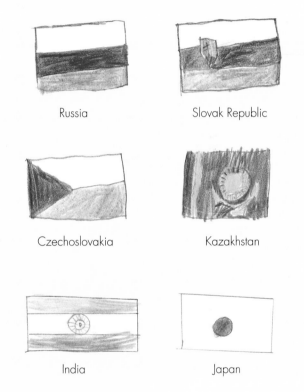

Russia

Slovak Republic

Czechoslovakia

Kazakhstan

India

Japan

at its base depicts artists. The marble statues at each corner symbolize Africa, Asia, Europe and America. During the two world wars German bombers used it as a landmark.

3. Cross Kensington Gore just opposite the Royal Albert Hall, one of the very few round (strictly speaking oval) buildings in London. Walk round the back of it and down some steps towards the Royal College of Music. Cross Prince Consort Road and turn left. Turn right into Exhibition Road and walk towards the Cromwell Road, past Imperial College and the Science Museum. As you are walking, imagine you are fourteen-year-old agent Alex Rider parachuting in on a mission to save the world and crashing through the roof of the Museum, as Alex did – and without serious injury! – at the end of the film *Stormbreaker*. Pop into the Museum for a pit stop and check out the cool spy stuff in the shop.

4. Turn left at the Cromwell Road and walk past the Victoria and Albert Museum to the Brompton Oratory, the second-largest Catholic church in London after Westminster Cathedral. This is the location of a KGB 'dead letter box' where, during the Cold War, espionage communications were dropped off to be collected without direct contact. The exact place the agents used was the gap behind the pillars to the left of the *pietà* statue of the Virgin Mary holding the dead Christ, tucked in a side chapel on the right-hand side just as you enter the church. Coming out of the church, turn left then left again down Cottage Place, through a car park, to the Holy Trinity Church. In the flower bed on the left is a large tree shading a statue of St Francis of Assisi, where agents used to hide microfilms. Walk back to the Brompton Road, towards the Oratory.

5. Cross over Thurloe Place at the lights and turn right – past the embassy of Kazakhstan – and then left into Thurloe Square. Turn right at the end, then left, crossing Pelham Street into Pelham Place. Then turn left into Pelham Crescent.

6. Turn left and cross the Fulham Road at the lights by the Michelin building (the Conran shop), then turn right down Sloane Avenue. Turn right down Petyward and then left into Elystan Street. Cross over Whiteheads Grove and Cale Street and continue along Markham Street until you hit the King's Road.

7. Cross straight over and turn left. Smith Street will soon be on your right. Stop here and look across the King's Road to see where the Cambridge Five – a ring of British men recruited into MI5 or MI6 at Cambridge University who became KGB moles and gave secrets to the Soviet Union – used to meet. Now a building society, it was then a pub called the Markham

Spy Jargon

Acorn a spy
Birdwatcher a spy
Cobbler a spy who creates false papers
Ears only material too secret to put in writing
Eyes only documents that may be read but not discussed
Honey trap an attractive person who entices someone into revealing secrets
Letterbox a go-between
Mole a spy working within an enemy intelligence agency
Pavement artist a spy who gathers intelligence on foot
Pocket litter receipts, coins, bus tickets, etc., that spies keep in their pockets to add authenticity to their false identity

Arms. The group comprised Kim Philby (cryptonym: Stanley); Donald Maclean (cryptonym: Homer), Guy Burgess (cryptonym: Hicks), Anthony Blunt (cryptonym: Johnson), who worked for the Queen (!) and John Cairncross (cryptonym: Liszt).

Keep going, passing Wellington Square, made famous as James Bond's suitably glamorous fictitious residence. Continue to Royal Avenue, then turn right. Ahead is the Royal Hospital, home of the British Army veterans known as Chelsea Pensioners.

8. Turn left into St Leonard's Terrace, the street used in *Stormbreaker* as the Chelsea home of Alex Rider. Walk to the end and turn left up Cheltenham Terrace back to the King's Road.

9. Turn right past the old Chelsea Barracks (now shops and the Saatchi Gallery), up to Sloane Square and the tube station.

Eat me, drink me
There's a good café at the Science Museum. Or you can picnic in the Royal Hospital grounds.

Useful information

- Kensington Palace State Apartments 0844 482 7799
  www.hrp.org.uk
- Science Museum 0870 870 4868 www.sciencemuseum.org.uk
- Victoria and Albert Museum 020 7942 2000 www.vam.ac.uk
- Brompton Oratory 020 7808 0900 www.bromptonoratory.com

Further afield

- The Imperial War Museum in Southwark, a museum about
  the history of twentieth-century war, has lots of interesting
  information about spies and spying. It also looks after
  Churchill's secret bunker and the Cabinet War Rooms at
  Whitehall. 020 7416 5000 www.iwm.org.uk
- You can see the Enigma machine at Bletchley Park, home of
  the World War II code cracking team in Milton Keynes.
  01908 640 404 www.bletchleypark.org.uk
- The Kelvedon Hatch Secret Nuclear Bunker in Essex
  012277 364883 www.secretnuclearbunker.com

Books to read

- Alex Rider series by Anthony Horowitz
- James Bond series by Ian Fleming

Did you know?

- In 1978 a journalist and Bulgarian dissident, Georgi Markov,
  was fatally stabbed with an umbrella impregnated with a lethal
  toxin, ricin, as he waited at a bus stop on Waterloo Bridge.
- On 23 November 2006 a Russian ex-KGB agent, Alexander
  Litvinenko, died after being mysteriously poisoned.
- During World War II people convicted of treason were
  executed by firing squad at the Tower of London.
- The MI6 headquarters at Vauxhall has a 'Faraday Cage' (a fine
  wire mesh) built into its framework making it impenetrable to
  electromagnetic information.

4. Great Expectations: Charles Dickens and a Victorian childhood

The Adventure

London is as much a part of Charles Dickens's own life as it is of his books. As a twelve-year-old boy he was forced to work in a blacking factory while his father served time in a debtors' prison in Southwark. It was an experience that deeply affected him, giving him an insight into the lives of the London poor. As a young man, he worked as a lawyer's clerk in the Inns of Court, before becoming a journalist. He spent hours every week simply walking the streets of London, sometimes fifteen miles at a time. He knew every inch of the city and he has woven the streets of London into the pages of his stories, with landmarks such as St Paul's Cathedral and London Bridge as a backdrop. Many places have changed or disappeared but many others still exist and can give that tingling feeling of stepping back in time into the pages of *Oliver Twist* or *Little Dorrit*.

Leaf through almost any Dickens novel and mark out London scenes to read before you go. Take along a copy of *Bleak House* and read the opening chapter to get yourselves in the spirit of foggy Victorian London.

How far? 6.4 km/4 miles
Start Russell Square tube **Finish** Farringdon tube

Walk the Walk

1. Turn right out of the tube and walk down Bernard Street, crossing over Grenville Street to Brunswick Square and on towards Coram's Fields. Follow the road round to the right at Lansdowne Terrace. Turn left on to Guilford Street.

2. Take the fourth turning on the right on to Doughty Street. Charles Dickens House is across the road at No. 48. This is where Dickens moved shortly after his marriage to his wife, Catherine Hogarth. They had ten children: Charles, Mary, Kate, Walter, Francis, Alfred, Sydney, Henry, Dora and Edward. While he was living

here, Dickens wrote some of his greatest novels, including *Nicholas Nickleby* and *Oliver Twist*. The house is now a museum with a small shop.

3. Leaving the house, turn left down Doughty Street and John Street to Theobald's Road. On weekday lunchtimes you are allowed to explore or picnic in Gray's Inn Gardens directly opposite. Dickens worked at Gray's Inn as a solicitor's clerk when he was fifteen. Otherwise, head right, cross Theobald's Road, take a left down Jockey's Fields and bend to the right on Bedford Row. Opposite a rather splendid old water pump in the middle of the road, turn left down Brownlow Street and out on to the bustle of High Holborn.

Turn left, cross at the lights, then immediately turn right into Chancery Lane. Walk down the hill to Fleet Street. To your right in the middle of Fleet Street is a statue of a dragon, guarding the entrance to the

Dickensian Words

Belcher a neckerchief
Blucher a shoe
Copper a large copper pan (or a penny)
Covey a mate, a bloke
Crib a cottage or house
Fogle hunter a pickpocket
Porter beer
Shaver a joker (usually a boy)
Smalls underwear
Stone jug prison
Strop piece of leather to sharpen razors on
Transport send (a criminal) to another country

City of London – the ancient divide between Roman and Saxon London, the City and Westminster. You are now officially in the City.

4. Cross over Fleet Street and look for a fabulous Tudor archway just across the road. Walk through here and into the hallowed space called the Temple, where the law has been served since the fourteenth century by the chambers of barristers on every stairwell. Walk through the arch and follow the gas-lit alleyway to Temple Church, the church of the Knights Templar, the soldier monks of the Crusades.

(If you are exploring at the weekend, this gate will be closed. Turn left, heading east down Fleet Street. Then turn right into Bouverie Street and enter the Temple through the Tudor Street Gate, about half-way down the hill, on the right. Turn right into the Temple and walk up the hill to the top. Turn left through an archway between the Library and the Francis Taylor Building. Walk through the courtyard to Temple Church.)

With the church door behind you, cross the courtyard and turn right through the pillars to the steps down to Elm Court. Walk through Elm Court and out on to a cobbled road. This is Middle Temple Lane. Walk straight across, past Middle Temple hall on your left. Here, in 1602, William Shakespeare's theatre troupe put on the first recorded performance of *Twelfth Night*.

Ahead of you is Fountain Court. Look for the fountain inscribed with a quote from Dickens's *Martin Chuzzlewit*. Tom Pinch worked here, in shambolic chambers. In *Great Expectations*, Pip lodged in the Temple. The beautifully preserved labyrinth of winding passages and open courtyards of the Temple is pretty much as it was when Dickens walked through it. Working as a solicitor's clerk, Dickens was always coming and going between Gray's Inn and the Temple. He didn't much like his job and entertained himself by throwing cherry stones out of the window at passers-by. But his experiences left their mark on his stories, many of which are rich with characters from both sides of the law.

Turn back past Middle Temple Hall and then right down Middle Temple Lane. Turn left through the archway towards

Inner Temple Gardens (open summer weekdays 12.30–3 p.m.). Keep straight on until you reach the Tudor Street Gate. Exit here and turn right on Temple Avenue. Cross over Victoria Embankment and turn left along the river.

5. Follow the path as it drops down below the road, signposted the Thames Path, heading east. Walk alongside the river until you reach the Millennium Footbridge. Turn left here and up the steps towards St Paul's Cathedral on Peter's Hill.

6. Cross at the traffic lights, noting the College of Arms on the left. Cross over to St Paul's Cathedral and head left around the steps of the Cathedral to the other side. Ahead is Temple Bar, the old arched entrance to the City, which used to stand on Fleet Street where the dragon is now.

7. Walk through Temple Bar into Paternoster Square. Turn left immediately down Paternoster Lane and right into Warwick Lane. Turn left on to Newgate Street, passing the site of Old Newgate Prison, demolished in 1777. Opposite the Old Bailey turn right on to Giltspur Street, passing St Sepulchre-without-Newgate church. Note the watchtower over the graveyard, built to guard the dead from bodysnatchers. Walk up Giltspur Street, alongside St Bartholomew's Hospital, into West Smithfield. Walk around the square to the right, towards the Tudor gateway of St Bartholomew's church, and take a right down Cloth Fair. Immediately turn left down Barley Mow Passage, through to Long Lane, and turn left.

8. You are now right outside Smithfield, London's famous meat market, the same market that Oliver Twist was taken through by Bill Sykes, early one morning. Imagine 'the bellowing and plunging of the oxen, the bleating of the sheep, the grunting and

Victorian Money

£1 otherwise known as a sovereign = twenty shillings
Guinea = twenty-one shillings
Half sovereign = ten shillings
Crown = five shillings
Half a crown = two shillings and sixpence
Florin = two shillings
Bob = one shilling
1 shilling = twelve pennies
Thrup'ny bit = three pennies
Copper = one penny

Victorian London

Being a child in Victorian London was not much fun. Ordinary children had a very hard life. They didn't go to school and often had to work from six in the morning to ten at night. Girls often worked as matchgirls or watercress and flower sellers in the markets, boys as chimney sweeps, street sweepers, mudlarks or street acrobats.

squeaking of pigs, the cries of hawkers, the shouts, the oaths, a bewildering scene, which quite confounded the senses'.

9. Turn right through the market, up the Grand Avenue. Cross Charterhouse Street and walk up St John Street. Opposite No. 88 turn left down a narrow passage called Passing Alley. Turn right and walk through St John's Gate. Cross over the Clerkenwell Road and walk straight up through St John's Square, leaving via Jerusalem Passage. Turn left down Aylesbury Street into Clerkenwell Green, where Oliver, with his friend the Artful Dodger, fatefully picks Mr Brownlow's pocket. Cross the road and walk diagonally through the churchyard of St James church and out at the far end on the left.

10. Turn right on to Clerkenwell Close. To the left is Pear Tree Court, site of Fagin's lair, a 'foul'd and frosty den, where vice is closely packed', now a Peabody Housing Estate. Cut left through here to the Betsey Trotwood pub, named after David Copperfield's aunt. Turn left down Farringdon Road and left on Cowcross Street to Farringdon tube station.

Eat me, drink me

There are cafés around Smithfield Market, good restaurants on St John Street and a mix of both pizza places and some of London's best restaurants on nearby Exmouth Market.

Tankard

Useful information

- Charles Dickens House 020 7405 2127
  www.dickensmuseum.com
- Temple Church 020 7353 3470 www.templechurch.com.
- Middle Temple Hall 020 7427 4800
  www.middletemple.org.uk.

Books to read

By Charles Dickens, in the order they were written:
*The Pickwick Papers, Oliver Twist, Nicholas Nickleby,
The Old Curiosity Shop, Barnaby Rudge, Martin Chuzzlewit,
A Christmas Carol, Dombey and Son, David Copperfield,
Bleak House, Hard Times, Little Dorrit, A Tale of Two Cities,
Great Expectations, Our Mutual Friend,
The Mystery of Edwin Drood*

Did you know?

- Charles Dickens is buried in Poets' Corner in Westminster
Abbey. He was buried in secret at night but his
grave was left open for the crowds who had
come to mourn. Over a thousand people
were still waiting to pay their respects when
they closed his grave two days later. It was
overflowing with flowers.

Victorian Street Urchin

- Henry Mayhew was a Victorian
journalist who interviewed Londoners,
including children, about their hard
lives. His articles were published in
a book called *London Labour and the
London Poor*. Dickens was a great admirer
of his work.

5. Paddington Bear and Portobello Market

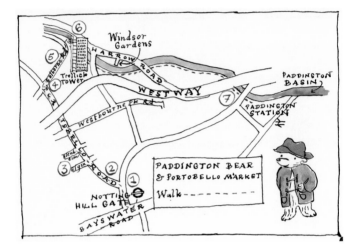

The Adventure

Paddington Bear, found at Paddington Station with a battered suitcase and a label around his neck saying 'Please look after this Bear, thank you', was taken home by the kind Brown family and has captured the hearts of children ever since. Not being the kind of bear to waste a good opportunity, Paddington would have loved the idea of exploring where he lived. Michael Bond set his adventures, scrapes and muddles in the area of west London around Paddington and Notting Hill. The Brown family home, 32 Windsor Gardens, is no longer there and the street is a disappointing cul-de-sac off the Harrow Road, but the charms of Portobello Road with its cake shops (for elevenses, buns and cocoa) and antique shops, just like Paddington's great friend Mr Gruber's with its 'rows of books and gleaming piles of copper and brass', are wonderful to explore at any age. The fruit and vegetable market at Portobello is open every day except Sunday. The crowded antiques market takes place only on Saturdays, but on other days there are still plenty of shops and some stalls to explore.

The walk ends along the canal through the high-class reclamation at Paddington Basin and the station, where there is a small statue of the bear. Pack a small suitcase, ideally with a secret compartment for important papers and a notebook, make a stack of marmalade sandwiches, give your children some bun money, and set off for the day.

How far? 4.8 km/3 miles
Start Notting Hill Gate tube **Finish** Paddington tube and rail

Walk the Walk

1. Leave by the exit on the north side of Notting Hill Gate and take the first right on to Pembridge Road.

2. Peel off at the second turning on the left into Portobello Road. If you are there for the antiques market (Saturdays), the stalls start properly where Chepstow Villas cross the Portobello Road and continue down to Elgin Crescent, about half a mile. On the next stretch of the Portobello Road, from Elgin Crescent to Talbot Road, the stalls sell fruit and vegetables, bread, cheese, cakes and croissants.

3. It is worth nipping left at Blenheim Crescent to take a look at the Travel Bookshop, star of the film *Notting Hill*. Next door is the charming Blenheim Bookshop and opposite is Books for Cooks, packed with cookbooks, where you can pick up a recipe for marmalade or buns. And they have a great café.

Carry on up Portobello Road. From Talbot Road to the Westway flyover (the motorway into London that passes overhead) are fashion stalls, with young designers selling their wares. As you go

Paddington

under the Westway, you leave the more elegant parts of the street behind. Here you are into the second-hand stalls, mostly clothes and bric-a-brac, all the way to Golborne Road.

4. Turn right on to Golborne Road and walk to the end, towards the Trellick Tower, a 31-storey tower block designed by the controversial architect Ernö Goldfinger and opened in 1972. Walk over the railway bridge.

5. Just before Trellick Tower, there is a mini roundabout. Go left here, pass the bottom of the Tower and immediately after it you will see Meanwhile Gardens and a footpath to the Grand Union Canal on the bend in the road. Turn right here.

6. Walk up to the canal and turn right on to the towpath. Keep walking. After the bridge look across the canal towards Windsor Gardens, Paddington's old street. Sadly, though, No. 32, where Paddington lived, no longer exists.

Paddington

Paddington was the kind of bear that things happened to. He was also a very helpful bear, which is why everyone forgave him when things went wrong. In the stories, he is, among many things, a detective, a magician, a decorator, and a chimney sweep. Think of your own Paddington story and how he might get out of a scrape or two of his own making. Sit by the canal and read a chapter of his adventures.

Practise your Paddington 'hard stare'

Make the crossest face you can possibly imagine and fix your eyes on the person who has upset you, without blinking, for as long as you can. Paddington usually saved his hard stares for Mr Curry, his mean-spirited neighbour.

7. Walk for about a mile to the charming Little Venice, where the Grand Union Canal joins the Regent's Canal. Keep straight on towards the offices of Paddington Basin. Stick to the canal side at Paddington Central, pass under the Westway flyover, then under Bishop's Bridge Road. On the right is a ramped path straight towards the domed roof of Paddington Station. Leaving the towpath, walk down here and follow the signs into the station. Once inside, look for the statue of Paddington outside Krispy Kreme Doughnuts. Gawp at the souvenirs at one of the dedicated Paddington Bear stands.

Eat me, drink me

Portobello Road is packed with some of London's most delightful bakeries, cafés and cake shops. Paddington would have been spoilt for choice, as you will be.

canal boat

Useful information
- Paddington Bear www.paddingtonbear.com
- Portobello Antiques Market www.portobelloroad.co.uk

Books to read
By Michael Bond:
A Bear Called Paddington, More About Paddington,
Paddington Helps Out, Paddington Abroad, Paddington
at Large, Paddington Marches On, Paddington at Work,
Paddington Goes to Town, Paddington Takes the Air,
Paddington on Top, Paddington Takes the Test, Paddington on
Screen, and many more.

Did you know?

- Michael Bond, the writer of the Paddington Bear stories, worked as a BBC cameraman on the children's programme *Blue Peter*.
- As his books became popular, a toy company called Gabrielle Designs created the first toy Paddington Bear. The sample was given to the owners' children for Christmas. One of the children was Jeremy Clarkson, of *Top Gear* fame.

Make Marmalade

Ingredients
1 kg Seville oranges • 2 lemons • 1.5 kg jam sugar

- There is a very small window for buying Seville oranges in London, usually just January. Halve the oranges and lemons, squeeze out the juice and pour it into your jam kettle.
- Keep the pips and pith and put them in a square of muslin, tie them up and add them to the pan.
- Cut the empty halves into slices. They will float in the finished marmalade. Add them to the pan.
- Pour in 2.8 litres of water and bring to the boil; reduce the heat and simmer for two hours.
- Add the sugar and stir well until the sugar dissolves. Then boil rapidly to setting point for about twenty more minutes. Test to see if the marmalade will set by dropping a spoonful on a very cold plate. If it wrinkles when you push it with your finger, it is done.
- Ladle into sterilized jam jars.
- Eat in sandwiches or with toast and butter at any time of day, just like Paddington Bear.

6. What the Romans did for London

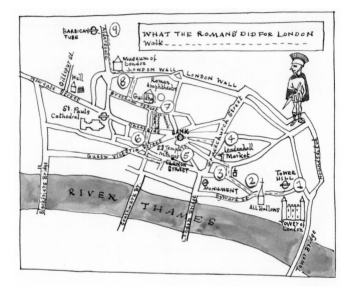

The Adventure

Before the Romans came there was no London, just fields and streams. Then, in AD 43, the Emperor Claudius commanded an invasion, bringing elephants to Britain to terrify the Celtic people. The site of London was chosen for a new town, close to fresh water, wood for building and access to the sea via the river. The Romans settled here to trade, importing wines, fish and olive oil and exporting wool, tin and slaves for the Roman Empire. They built the first bridge across the Thames, a walled city, and a network of roads that connected Londinium to the rest of Britain. During the Roman occupation, which lasted four hundred years, London was an important trading city.

Everything you see in the square mile of the City today has been built on the ruins of the old Roman site. Only fragments remain, but when you come across them, they are so precious they take your breath away. Londinium was wealthy. It had a vast basilica and city hall, imposing stone buildings, bathhouses, temples, a fort, an amphitheatre and a market place. The Romans brought civilization with them. As John Cleese says in the Monty Python film *Life of Brian*, what have the Romans ever done for us? Well, they brought sanitation, medicine, education, wine, public order, irrigation, roads. They gave us the City of London.

How far? 4 km/2½ miles
Start Tower Hill tube **Finish** Barbican tube

Walk the Walk

1. Leave Tower Hill tube, following the signs to the Tower of London and heading down the steps under the roadway. Halfway down, take a left to see a stunning section of the Roman city wall. This is the most impressive surviving part, dating back to AD 200. In front of it is a statue of the Roman Emperor Trajan (reigned AD 98–117).

   Walk down the rest of the steps and through the underpass, where there is another section of wall in a well just in front of the Tower. Take a right and head up the ramp towards the Tower of London ticket office. Keep going straight on past this, leaving it on your left, towards the church of All Hallows by the Tower, the oldest church in the City.

2. Go in and find the Undercroft at the back, through the Brass Rubbing Centre. There is a museum in the crypt, stuffed with Roman and Saxon artefacts. Note the Saxon arch as you go downstairs: the darker red tiles are Roman.

At the bottom of the stairs is a haunting section of tessellated pavement, probably the floor of a Roman house. Further into the crypt there is a model of Roman London, a good way to see the City as it was then. Dotted through the crypt are artefacts, cornices and squared stones from Roman buildings. Many were found in a thick layer of ash, evidence of the fire started by the Celtic warrior queen Boudicca when she razed Londinium to the ground in AD 61, killing tens of thousands of citizens. It was her ferocious attack that led the Romans to build a vast wall 6m/20ft high around the City.

Leave the church by the opposite door and turn right, heading for the traffic lights across the busy Byward Street. Cross here then cross to the other side of Great Tower Street. Walk left up Great Tower Street towards St Margaret Pattens church.

3.   When you reach the church, turn right up Rood Lane. At the end, turn left on to Fenchurch Street, then immediately right on to Lime Street and left into Lime Street Passage and Leadenhall Market. Take the first left through a passageway called Bull's Head Passage. Turn right on to Gracechurch Street.

Some Roman Gods

Jupiter	King of the gods, he hurled a thunderbolt when he was angry
Juno	Goddess of women
Venus	Goddess of love and beauty
Diana	Goddess of hunting
Bacchus	God of wine and feasting,
Mercury	Messenger of the gods, with a winged helmet
Vesta	Goddess of the home
Mars	God of war
Mithras	God of light
Neptune	God of the sea

This area, between Leadenhall Street and Fenchurch Street, was the site of some of the grandest buildings in Roman London, the Basilica (the Roman city hall) and the Forum (the market). The Museum of London has a fascinating scale model of how this would have looked.

4. Walk up Gracechurch Street to Nicholson and Griffin hairdressers at No. 90. If you ask, they will take you downstairs and show you the only surviving part of the Roman Basilica. Cross over Gracechurch Street and cut into the alley Corbet Court, ahead of you. Walk up the steps and round the back of St Michael's churchyard. Walk right, around the railings, then straight on through the alleyway Castle Court, coming out at Birchin Lane. Turn left on Birchin Lane and right into Change Alley, following this passage all the way to the end. Then turn left.

5. Turn right on Lombard Street and walk around the front of St Mary Woolnoth church. Cross King William Street and head

Roman coin

straight down St Swithin's Lane to Cannon Street. Turn right and note the London Stone, sadly entombed in the wall behind a railing. Some say this is a Roman *millarium*, a milestone that marked the central point from where all road distances were measured. Cannon Street is where traces of the grandest Roman buildings have been found, including the governor's palace, with its gardens, water pools and mosaics. Cross over at the station and turn left on to Dowgate Hill, then immediately right on to Cloak Lane.

6. Walk on and turn right at Queen Street. Cross Cannon Street again at the lights, walking up to Queen Victoria Street. Turn right here and walk a short way to some hoarding on the right and the ruins of a Roman temple for the worship of Mithras, a god whose code emphasized honour, truth and courage. This temple was moved here from Walbrook, where it was discovered during building work in 1954. It was once underground and the Romans would have held candlelit feasts and rituals inside it. The Museum of London has exquisite sculptures taken from the temple.

Retrace your steps and turn right at the traffic lights up Queen Street. Look out to your left for Watling Street, a section of Roman road, and the site of the Roman fort in London. Cross Cheapside. Turn right, then immediately left up the tiny Ironmonger Lane. Ring the bell at No. 11. If the security guard is in (Monday to Friday), ask to see the precious Roman mosaic in the basement. He will take you downstairs to an empty basement with a beautiful faded section of a Roman mosaic floor with red, blue, yellow and white flowers.

7. Turn left into Gresham Street and then right towards the magnificent Guildhall, the City's civic centre. On your right is the Guildhall Art Gallery and below it is one of the treasures of London, a Roman amphitheatre. Discovered during building works in 1988, just fragmented sections are left but the display

has been constructed with imagination and care, and the effect is powerful. The lights are dim and the crowds cheer as you approach the cobbled passage that was used by gladiators and wild animals to enter the arena. Leave by crossing Guildhall Yard and turning right on to Gresham Street. Turn right on to Wood Street, passing the tower of St Alban in the middle of the road.

8. Just before you reach London Wall, a busy road, you will come to an escalator. Take the escalator up and follow the signs to the Museum of London, passing some of the best views of the last remaining stretches of the Roman Wall below the walkway. At the top, bend left and go straight on to the Museum. The collection of Roman artefacts here comprises 47,000 objects recovered during building in and around

London. Exhibits include mosaic floors, ceramics, leather shoes, and a Roman bikini.

9. When you are ready, head up Aldersgate to Barbican tube.

Eat me, drink me

The Museum of London café is great. Or have a picnic on the grass below the museum underneath the Roman wall.

Useful information

- Museum of London 020 7001 9844
  www.museumoflondon.org.uk
- The Roman amphitheatre at Guildhall Art Gallery
  020 7332 3700 www.cityoflondon.gov.uk

Further afield

England is rich with Roman remains. Head north to Hadrian's Wall and the Roman forts (www.english-heritage.org.uk) or plan a walk from end to end (www.hadrians-wall.org). Visit the Roman baths in Bath (www.romanbaths.co.uk) or, closer to London, the Verulamium Museum in St Albans (www.stalbansmuseums.org.uk).

Books to read

- *The Eagle of the Ninth* by Rosemary Sutcliff (OUP)
- *The Roman Mysteries* by Caroline Lawrence (Orion)

Did you know?

- The Romans didn't have toilet paper; they used a wet sponge on a stick instead.
- The 1500-year-old remains of a Roman teenage girl were found in front of the Gherkin when it was being built in 2003. She was given a Roman burial.
- On the corner of Giltspur Street is a Merrill Lynch office which under the building has a section of Roman Wall with the River Fleet running through it.

7. Time and Space at Greenwich

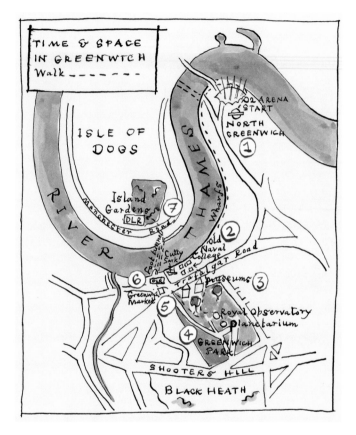

The Adventure

Greenwich commands the river approach to the capital and is steeped in London's royal, naval and scientific history. The long association between Greenwich and the navy began under the Tudor monarchs: Henry VIII established naval dockyards at nearby

Deptford and Woolwich and Elizabeth I made Greenwich Palace the scene of great festivals, including launch parties for many voyages of exploration. It was here that Queen Elizabeth I signed the orders that sent out her fleet against the Spanish Armada.

Today, the site is divided between the National Maritime Museum, the Royal Observatory (including the Peter Harrison Planetarium), and the Old Royal Naval College, all of which boast spectacular architecture. Stand on the Greenwich Meridian Line, with one foot in the eastern and one in the western hemisphere. See and learn about the stars and how they help sailors navigate the high seas. Take binoculars to survey the boats and birds on the river and sing some sea shanties as you go.

How far? 8 km/5 miles (short version 3.2 km/2 miles)
Start North Greenwich tube **Finish** Island Gardens DLR station

Walk the Walk

1. Come up the escalator and leave by the exit behind you in the direction of the Millennium Dome (O2). Keeping the Dome to your left, head to the river, which you are going to follow for a couple of miles, through a brooding landscape of warehouse buildings, piers and slow-moving cargo barges. If you've got very little legs you might find this stretch a bit far, in which case you can take a Thames Clipper, to arrive at Greenwich by boat, as many a great sea captain has done before you.

At the waterfront turn left, going westwards, passing along the way a number of wharves: Ordnance, Delta, Primrose, Morden, Enderby's, Piper's, Granite and Lovell's. Keep following the signs for the Thames Path as it wiggles around the warehouses all the way to Greenwich. Keep binoculars handy for sightings of cormorants, grey heron, shelduck, red shank and grey-leg geese. The Thames, which in 1957 was

declared biologically dead, is now one of the cleanest rivers in Europe and has more than 125 species of fish. In 2006 a 5m/18ft Northern Bottlenose Whale swam upstream.

As the cream-coloured buildings of Greenwich get closer see how the river bends in a huge loop – you've probably seen it on a map before but it's quite something in real life. Take in the imposing Canary Wharf skyline across the river. You will soon arrive at Ballast Quay and the wonderful bow-fronted Cutty Sark pub. In the 1800s this quay was one of the busiest in the world.

Carry on and you will pass one more big warehouse building, dwarfing Trinity Hospital, the oldest surviving building in Greenwich, which provides alms to the elderly.

2. Greenwich comes to life at this point. Keep going straight on down Crane Street and at the end of the alleyway turn right down towards the river to inspect the statue of Lord Nelson and the Trafalgar pub, famous in the nineteenth century for its 'whitebait suppers'. Members of Parliament used to travel up the river to enjoy eating the whitebait fresh from the Thames.

Keep going along the river front and turn left into the Old Royal Naval College at the grand Water Gate. Originally the Royal Hospital for Seamen, it was built on the site of Greenwich Palace, Henry VIII's favourite and the birthplace of Elizabeth I. The original design was by Sir Christopher Wren, who laid the foundation stone in 1696. The Hospital was closed in 1869 and the building became the Navy's university. It now houses the University of Greenwich and the Trinity College of Music.

Walk through the green and into the spectacular Painted Hall, on the right. It took artist James Thornhill a staggering nineteen years to complete the painting, for which he was paid by the yard. The seamen who lived here took their meals of bread, beer and boiled meat in the undercroft below. The Wren chapel on the left is where Lord Nelson lay in state after his victorious death at the Battle of Trafalgar.

3. With the river in front of you, turn right to exit on to Park Row. Turn right, cross Romney Road and enter Greenwich Park on the corner. Walk towards the Queen's House, built by Inigo Jones and full of great art, including paintings of Cook's Pacific voyages and the famous Turner painting of the Battle of Trafalgar.

Walk through the colonnade, past the National Maritime Museum with its extensive collections, including thousands of

sea charts and maps dating from the medieval period, showing the results of exploration and discovery and demonstrating how techniques of navigation and surveying developed. This is a good moment to take a break, either in the café or on the grass, before you tackle the hill.

4. Climb up the steepish hill to the Royal Observatory and set your watch to Greenwich Mean Time while standing on the Meridian Line at 0 degrees longitude. Every place on earth is measured in terms of its distance east or west from here and it divides the eastern and western hemispheres. Astronomers use this arbitrary north–south line as a zero point from which to take measurements, making it possible to build up an accurate map of the night sky. The Observatory dates back to the reign of Charles II, when the impetus for learning about the stars was the need to discover a means for sailors to determine their longitude (east–west position) at sea.

A few steps further up the hill is the Peter Harrison Planetarium, with Europe's first digital laser planetarium projector, which allows the audiences out into space to look back at the earth.

Make a compass using the sun

You will need the sun to be shining strongly enough to cast a shadow for this to work. It is useful to remember that the sun rises in east and sets in the west, and at midday (in the northern hemisphere) it will be roughly south.

- Find a stick 1m/39in long and a flat piece of ground.
- Hold the stick at a 90 ° angle.
- Mark the tip of the stick's shadow with a stone or a stick or whatever you can find (call this A).
- Wait 30 minutes and repeat (call this B).
- Draw a line from point A to point B.
- This line will run from west to east, A being west, B being east.

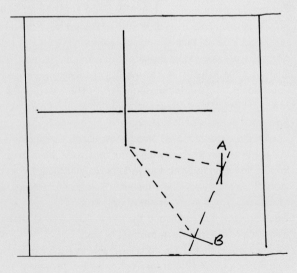

The museum tells you everything you need to know about the stars and the planets.

5. Run back down the hill and leave the park at St Mary's Gate in the westerly corner, near a statue of King William IV and opening out on to King William Walk. Walk down to Romney Road, cross over and go straight on. Turn left down Turpin Lane and pop into Greenwich Market. Exit the way you came in, turn left and and head towards the *Cutty Sark*: the fastest tea clipper of its day and the only 'extreme' clipper still in existence; it is currently under restoration.

6. Cross College Approach and turn left to the small glass-domed building on the water's edge to take the lift down to the Greenwich foot tunnel. A shaft 13.5m/44ft deep leads to the 371m/1217ft-long tunnel that runs under the Thames. If the tide is in when you pass through, you will be 16m/53ft under water.

7. Come out of the tunnel on the Isle of Dogs, cross Manchester Road to Island Gardens DLR station and take the train to Canary Wharf, where you can pick up the tube. This ride is an event in itself.

Eat me, drink me
Children are allowed in the upstairs bar and garden at the Cutty Sark Tavern (020 8858 3146). Or you can try one of the good cafés in the museums and the park. Or enjoy a picnic.

Useful information
- National Maritime Museum, Royal Observatory and Planetarium 020 8858 4422 www.nmm.ac.uk
- *Cutty Sark* 020 8858 2698 www.cuttysark.org.uk
- Greenwich Market is open Wednesday to Sunday www.greenwichmarket.net

Books to read
- *This Morning I Met a Whale* by Michael Morpurgo and Christian Birmingham. A charming story about the day a whale swam up the Thames.
- *Admiral Nelson: The Sailor Who Dared All to Win* by Sam Llewellyn. The story of Nelson's life.

Did you know?
- The earth spins counter-clockwise, rotating from west to east, which gives the impression that the sun rises and sets, but actually the sun does not move.
- A bell called the Lutine Bell is rung at Lloyds of London when a missing ship is reported.

Sing a Sea Shanty

My bonnie lies over the ocean,
My bonnie lies over the sea,
My bonnie lies over the ocean,
O bring back my bonnie to me.

(Chorus)
Bring back, bring back,
O, bring back my bonnie, to me, to me.
Bring back, bring back,
O, bring back my bonnie to me.

Last night as I lay on my pillow,
Last night as I lay on my bed,
Last night as I lay on my pillow,
I dreamed that my bonnie was dead.

O blow ye winds over the ocean,
O blow ye winds over the sea,
O blow ye winds over the ocean,
And bring back my bonnie to me.

The winds have blown over the ocean,
The winds have blown over the sea,
The winds have blown over the ocean,
And brought back my bonnie to me.

8. Poetry on Hampstead Heath

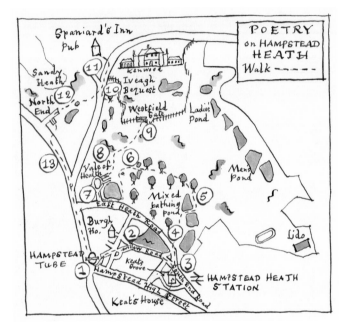

The Adventure

Ever since the eighteenth century, when Dr Gibbons declared Hampstead's spa waters of medicinal value, people have flocked here. The village, with its steep high street, elegant houses, shops, cafés and wealthy inhabitants, feels a world away from central London, but is actually only a few stops up the Northern Line.

The Heath is Hampstead's prize. The wildness and beauty of its 800 acres of hills and heath, so close to the centre of one of the world's greatest cities is a great luxury for London. It is also one of London's most literary places. Some of England's greatest poets, artists and writers have lived nearby, or have been inspired by the

Heath. John Keats, Percy Bysshe Shelley, Samuel Coleridge, John Constable, Charles Dickens, H.G. Wells, Katherine Mansfield, D.H. Lawrence and many others have all been drawn to the Heath.

Bring your costumes to swim in the bathing ponds, walk through the woods, climb trees, go fishing, float boats on the water, like the young Shelley, and have a picnic in the long meadow grass.

How far? 4.8 km/3 miles
Start and finish Hampstead tube

Walk the Walk

1. Turn left out of the station on to Hampstead High Street and shortly left into the narrow, shop-fronted Flask Walk. Carry straight on downhill, passing a double red telephone box. Set back, up on the left on the corner of New End Square, is Burgh House, now the home of the Hampstead Museum. Rudyard Kipling's daughter Elsie once lived in this house, and Kipling often visited.

2. Turn right on to Willow Road and walk all the way around the corner to No. 2, a 1930s modernist house built by architect Ernö Goldfinger as his family home. Now owned by the National Trust, it is a style guru's paradise. The rooms are flanked with works by artists including Man Ray and Henry Moore. James Bond's enemy was named after this Goldfinger. Ian Fleming, who lived around the corner, reputedly detested him.

3. The Heath is now beginning to emerge to your left. Cross over Downshire Hill and carry on straight along South End Road. Turn right into Keats Grove to take a look at the tragically romantic (and newly restored) Keats House, shortly on the left. This is where the young John Keats lived from 1818 to 1820 and where he fell in love with Fanny Brawne, the girl next door. Inside, you can see the engagement ring he secretly gave to Fanny, and the

Dog Rose

bed he slept in when he first became ill with tuberculosis. He left Hampstead for Rome and warmer weather on doctor's advice, but died just months later, aged twenty-five.

4. Retrace your steps down Keats Grove but this time cross over South End Road. A path heads left on to the Heath. Follow this and you will soon pass the first of several ponds on your right. Take the path across the second pond. To your left is the mixed-bathing pond where you can brave wild swimming in the summer months. Men-only and women-only ponds are to be found on the other side of the Heath.

5. Immediately after this, turn left off the main path on to a smaller one, then fork right up into the trees. At the top, this path joins a tarmac path. Turn left and follow the path through the woods. The Heath is wooded to the left, with lots of trees to climb and

FLOWERS

Bramble

Buttercup

Cowslip

Daisy

Devil's-bit Scabious

Dog Rose

Elderflower

Heather

Purple Loosestrife

explore. At the crossroads of paths, carry straight on. Shortly you reach an old stone bridge above another pond; the path carries on uphill through the Heath. Keep to the main path, climbing gently and eventually passing some mock-Tudor toilets discreetly hidden behind some bushes.

6. Just ahead, to the left of the path, is a round ice-house. Keeping the ice-house on your left, head off the main path here, down a small path towards some fairground caravans.

7. At the bottom, turn left towards another pond. Walk around it and turn right up the muddy path around the back of it. This would be a good pond to fish in (you need a licence); or you could float paper boats, as Shelley once did here. Follow the path into the trees towards the Vale of Health, a collection of cottages and villas. Turn right at the road and walk through the houses, looking out for literary plaques as you go. Wiggle through until you come to the end and face the Heath again.

Ode to a Nightingale

My heart aches, and a drowsy numbness pains
My sense, as though of hemlock I had drunk,
Or emptied some dull opiate to the drains
One minute past, and Lethe-wards had sunk:
'Tis not through envy of thy happy lot,
But being too happy in thine happiness,
That thou, light-winged Dryad of the trees,
In some melodious plot
Of beechen green, and shadows numberless,
Singest of summer in full-throated ease.

This poem was written by Keats in his Hampstead garden while he listened to the nightingales singing on the Heath.

8. Turn right here, along the front of a row of houses. At the fence end, continue on a gravel path and then turn left on to a tarmac path that leads up the hill. At the top is an open green, with a path ahead on the far side of the clearing. Cut across the grass and pick up the path ahead, turning left into the woods steeply down to the bottom and up the other side again, keeping straight on.

9. The path is now wide and wooded, littered with great fallen trunks. Keep going straight until you reach the fence of the Iveagh Bequest, the more formal section of Hampstead Heath with its grand art gallery and café in Kenwood House. Look for the Westfield Gate to your right. Go through it and take the left path. Soon you are in open common, with long grass and wildflower meadows in the early summer.

write an ode

- Take a pen and paper with you to the Heath. Lie in the long grass and write an ode of your own.
- Think of something, or someone, you would like to praise or celebrate. Be as heartfelt as possible.
- Once you have a subject, write verses that are ten lines long, using the iambic pentameter as your rhythm. This means there are ten beats in a line and it goes something like deDUM, deDUM, deDUM, deDUM, deDUM.
- Make the end of the lines rhyme like this: ababcdecde.

10. Over the brow of the hill is a large fallen tree trunk. Turn left here and head up the hill into the woods, towards a 1960s block of flats at the top. Turn right and walk between the fences up to the road ahead. Leave the Heath through Ikin Gate.

11. If you want a pub stop, turn right at Spaniards Road and head for the Spaniards Inn, where Black Bess was reputedly stabled for Dick Turpin, and where the poets and artists of Hampstead would meet. If not, cross the zebra crossing and turn right. Turn immediately sharp left on a path into the Heath Extension, following it all the way down to the pond. The Heath feels different here, with gorse bushes and fewer trees.

12. Pass the pond and follow the path as it veers right down the hill, with a wooden fence in front of you, towards the houses and a small road called North End. Walk down the street. Turn left on North End Avenue and then back on to the Heath as the road becomes a path again.

13. At the top, turn right towards the red brick houses and the main road. Turn left on North End Way and walk back down the hill, straight over the roundabout, past the pond and downhill on Heath Street all the way to the shops in Hampstead Village. Take the tube at Hampstead.

Eat me, drink me

The Spaniards Inn is a decent pub with good food and a garden. 020 8731 8406 www.thespaniardshampstead.co.uk On the stretch of High Street down the hill from the tube are dozens of cafés and family-friendly restaurants. Or enjoy a picnic in the meadows on the Heath.

Useful information

- Hampstead Mixed Pond, swimming season from May to September, £2 adult, £1 child, children under eight not allowed
- You can fish in the ponds, except in the closed season (15 March to 15 June). Under-twelves can fish without a rod licence. You will also need a free permit from the tennis hut at Parliament Hill, on the other side of the heath.
- Hampstead Heath www.hampsteadheath.net
- Keats House 020 7332 3868 www.cityoflondon.gov.uk

Books to read

- *The New Penguin Book of Romantic Poetry* edited by Jonathan Wordsworth
- *The Woman in White* by Wilkie Collins. A nineteenth-century thriller that starts in Hampstead.

Did you know?

- Keats was a Londoner: he was born in a pub at Moorgate where his father worked as a barman.
- Keats trained and qualified as an apothecary surgeon.

meadow brown butterfly

9. 101 Dalmatians in Regent's Park

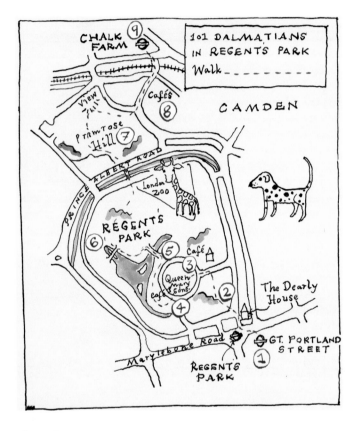

The Adventure

The 101 Dalmatians is Dodie Smith's story of two Dalmatians, Pongo and Missis Pongo (Perdita in the film) and their pets, Mr and Mrs Dearly. In the original 1956 book, Mr Dearly is a financial whizz who has wiped out the National Debt, and by way of thanks the Government has decreed that he never has to pay

A dalmation

tax again. In the film, he is transformed into the rather less affluent Roger Radcliffe, a struggling musician and composer. However they both live on the Outer Circle of Regent's Park in a grand house that can be identified in real life as 1 St Andrew's Place. Both versions of the story have a role for the evil, rich, Cruella de Vil, with half her hair black and half white, who steals the Pongos' Dalmatian puppies to make herself a fine fur coat.

This walk takes you from the house through Regent's Park, passing the pond and bridge where, in the film, bachelors Roger and Pongo meet their loves, Anita and Perdita. For an authentic recreation of the movie, go in early spring when the park is full of daffodils. Pass London Zoo and walk up to the top of Primrose Hill, where the dogs spread the word about the missing puppies at Twilight Barking and discover that they have been taken to the country. And here the adventure begins as the Dalmatians set off in search of the lost puppies; they finally bring them home, along with scores of others, to the Dearly/Radcliffe household.

How far? 4.8 km/3 miles
Start Great Portland Street tube **Finish** Chalk Farm tube

Walk the Walk

1. Leave the tube by the exit on the south side of the Marylebone Road. Cross over the busy road at the lights in front of you, and turn left. Cross Albany Street.

2. Turn right through the gates of the park on to Park Square East. As you walk up, there is a small dead-end turning on the right called St Andrew's Place, just by the Royal College of Physicians. No. 1 is the house where Pongo lived. Every day he and his master would take a walk in the park. It is worth looping around the pretty houses here, with their tidy black railings and characteristic lamp-posts.

Cross over the Outer Circle and enter Regent's Park through the gates on the corner into Avenue Gardens. Take the middle path, leading diagonally across the Gardens. The spring bulbs are particularly beautiful, with daffodils and crocus in March, just as in the Walt Disney film. Times have changed and no dogs are allowed in this part of the park, unfortunately. They are allowed in the wilder areas from no. 5 onwards. (See www.royalparks.org.uk, or look at the map board on the gate).

Turn right on to the Broad Walk with its urns and fountains and follow the line of trees to Chester Road at the top. Enjoy wandering through while the children dart between the topiary and the formal hedging.

3. When you reach Chester Road, turn left and walk along the road towards the golden gates. Crossing the Inner Circle, go

DOGS

Basset Hound

Cocker Spaniel

Jack Russell

Labrador

Miniature Schnauzer

St Bernard

Regent's Park

The land that became Regent's Park was once used by Henry VIII as a hunting chase. In 1811 the Prince Regent (later George IV) commissioned architect John Nash to build a summer palace here, complete with royal gardens and grand villas. But the Prince changed his mind and the palace was never built. The park was opened to the public in 1835, at first for just two days a week.

through the gates and turn left immediately into Queen Mary's Rose Garden, one of the finest collections of roses in England. Look out for the extraordinary names of the roses.

Ahead is a pond with ducks, willow trees and a little island to explore. Follow the path around the pond. Look for the arched bridge: this is the spot where Pongo fell in love – and into the pond.

4. The path leads to a wide, straight avenue, with a café ahead of you. Turn left, walking out of the gate and on to the Inner Circle. Turn right and walk around the road until you reach the stage door for the Open Air Theatre.

5. Cross the road here and turn left into the open, wilder parkland. Cross over Longbridge. This is a grazing area for birds. Look out for dogs and their owners. See if you can tell which types of dogs they are. Do the dogs and their owners share any characteristics? Look carefully. Turn left after the bridge and follow the path all the way, heading around the boating lake, and ending up at a Dairy Ices Shack. You can hire a boat at the lake here.

Mallard

6. There are three paths to the right here. Take the middle one, signposted London Zoo and

Primrose Hill Bridge. Walk across the park until you reach the Zoo. Cross the Outer Circle and over the canal, glimpsing the animals and Lord Snowdon's grand aviary as you pass.

7. Cross over Prince Albert Road at the zebra crossing and walk into Primrose Hill. Sticking to the path on the left-hand edge, walk straight up the hill. Then as you come up to the very top of the hill turn to the right. At 78m/256ft high Primrose Hill is one of the highest points in London. Take in the glorious views and imagine the Twilight Barking across London that led to the tracking down of the Dalmatian puppies. This is where it all happened.

8. With the Viewpoint sign in front of you, take the path diagonally downhill on your left to the gate at the bottom. Cross Primrose Hill Road to Regent's Park Road for a drink in a café or a browse in Primrose Hill Books. There is also a pet shop here for dog treats.

9. Keep going straight down Regent's Park Road. Cross King Henry's Road and walk over the footbridge. Turn right on Adelaide Road and you will shortly come to Chalk Farm tube station on your left.

Eat me, drink me
There are good cafés at several spots in Regent's Park. Otherwise, there are cafés and cake shops on Regent's Park Road. Or for one of the best ice-creams in London head for Marine Ices, opposite Chalk Farm tube. 020 7482 9003 www.marineices.co.uk

Useful information
- Regent's Park 020 7486 7905 www.royalparks.org.uk
- ZSL London Zoo, Regent's Park 020 7722 3333 www.zsl.org
- Open Air Theatre, Inner Circle, Regent's Park
  0844 826 4242 www.openairtheatre.org

Books to read
By Dodie Smith:
The 101 Dalmatians and *The Starlight Barking*

Did you know?
- Dodie Smith also wrote the fabulously romantic bestseller *I Capture the Castle*.
- In the Disney film, Pongo has 72 spots, Perdita has 68 spots and each puppy has 32 spots.
- A.A. Milne's Winnie-the-Pooh was called after Christopher Robin's teddy Winnie, which in turn was named for an American black bear called Winnipeg that Christopher Robin loved to visit in London Zoo.

10. Kings and Queens: London's Great Palaces

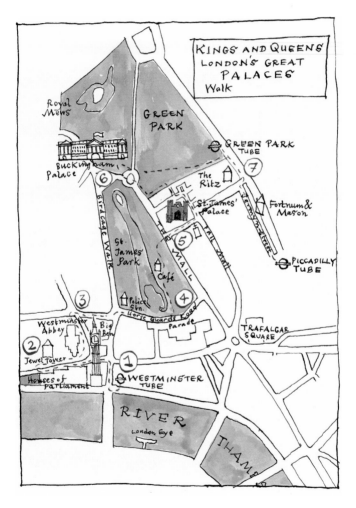

KINGS AND QUEENS
LONDON'S GREAT
PALACES
Walk

Royal Mews

GREEN PARK

⊖ GREEN PARK TUBE

⑦

Buckingham Palace

⑥

The Ritz

Fortnum & Mason

St. James' Palace

⑤

Birdcage Walk

St. James' Park

Café

The Mall

⊖ PICCADILLY TUBE

③

Westminster Abbey

Police Stn.

④

Horse Guards Road

Parade

TRAFALGAR SQUARE

②

Big Ben

Jewel Tower

①

Houses of Parliament

⊖ WESTMINSTER TUBE

RIVER

London Eye

THAMES

The Adventure

Be a prince or princess for the day and explore three royal palaces in one walk through history, from the Thames to Green Park. The first is the heart of English politics and power, the Palace of Westminster, now home to the British Government but during the Middle Ages a royal palace. Opposite the Houses of Parliament is the Jewel Tower, one of few remains of the medieval palace. It is a pocket-sized castle keep perfect for a child-sized spoonful of history. Cut through St James's Park, catching the soldiers preparing for the Changing of the Guard at Horse Guards Parade, heading towards the more humble St James's Palace, tucked away behind The Mall, with its fine chapel. Peer through the railings of Buckingham Palace or take the tour of some of its gold-edged, eyebrow-raising interiors. Then head across Green Park for tea at the Ritz or a knickerbocker glory at Fortnum and Mason, grocers to the royal family for centuries.

How far? 4 km/2½ miles
Start Westminster tube **Finish** Green Park tube

Walk the Walk

1. Follow the signs out of the station to exit 1, Westminster Pier. You are greeted with great views of the river and the London Eye. Climb the steps and pop out just opposite Big Ben. Cross Bridge Street and turn right. Along the river front is the Palace of Westminster, now the Houses of Parliament, but between the eleventh and sixteenth centuries home to the kings and queens of England. From 1265, when a parliament was created with two houses, the House of Lords met at the Palace of Westminster, but the House of Commons was not given a permanent home here till 1547. However, the building you are looking at is not the original Palace. This was destroyed by a terrible fire in 1834 and replaced by the present building, designed by Sir Charles Barry and his assistant Augustus Welby Pugin.

Look out for the taxi light on the corner of the building, lit when a Member of Parliament needs a cab. Walk around the front of the building, turning left on Parliament Square. Collect the names of the statues as you go. Look out for Oliver Cromwell, Winston Churchill, Nelson Mandela, Richard the Lionheart, Emmeline Pankhurst and George V. At the far end of the building is the Sovereign's Entrance, where the Queen enters once a year, in September, as part of the ceremony of the State Opening of Parliament.

2. Cross the main road at the crossing by Victoria Tower Gardens and double back to see the Jewel Tower. This tower is a perfect place for little ones to get a sense of history. Part of the original medieval palace, it was built in about 1365 as Edward III's privy wardrobe and treasure house. It was once surrounded by a moat, both to protect it and to provide fish for the table. The Jewel Tower, Westminster Hall and the crypt and cloisters of St Stephen's are all that is left of the medieval palace.

Kings and Queens of England

The Normans
William I 1066–1087
William II 1087–1100
Henry I 1100–1135
Stephen 1135–1154

The Plantagenets
Henry II 1154–1189
Richard I 1189–1199
John I 1199–1216
Henry III 1216–1272
Edward I 1272–1307
Edward II 1307–1327
Edward III 1327–1377
Richard II 1377–1399

The House of Lancaster
Henry IV 1399–1413
Henry V 1413–1422
Henry VI 1422–1461,
    1470 –1471

The House of York
Edward IV 1461–1470,
    1471–1483
Edward V 1483
Richard III 1483–1485

The Tudors
Henry VII 1485–1509

Henry VIII 1509–1547
Edward VI 1547–1553
[Lady Jane Grey 1553]
Mary I 1553–1558
Elizabeth I 1558–1603

The Stuarts
James I 1603–1625
Charles I 1625–1649
[Interregnum 1649–1660]
Charles II 1660–1685
James II 1685–1688
William III 1689–1702 and
    Mary II 1689–1694
Anne 1702–1714

House of Hanover
George I 1714–1727
George II 1727–1760
George III 1760–1820
George IV 1820–1830
William IV 1830–1837
Victoria 1837–1901

**Saxe-Coburg-Gotha and
    The House of Windsor**
Edward VII 1901–1910
George V 1910–1936
Edward VIII 1936
George VI 1936–1952
Elizabeth II 1952–today

If you can't remember all that, try this rhyme to help you memorize them:

Willie, Willie, Harry, Steve
Harry, Dick, John, Harry Three.
Edward One, Two, Three, Dick Two
Henry Four, Five, Six then who?
Edward Four, Five, Dick the bad
Harry's twain and Ned the lad.
Mary, Lizzie, James the vain
Charlie, Charlie, James again.
William and Mary, Anne O'Gloria,
Four Georges, William and Victoria
Edward Seven, Georgie Five,
Edward, George and Liz (alive).

Walk out of the Keep and turn left, leaving by the back gate of the Jewel Tower. Turn left again, and walk up the side of Westminster Abbey alongside St Margaret's church.

The Abbey was established by Edward the Confessor and was built as a place for the coronation and burial of kings and queens. It has been the setting for every royal coronation since 1066. Entrance is through the Great North Door, if you want to go in. St Margaret's church is free and worth visiting.

3. Walk around to the West Door, admiring the statues of ten twentieth-century martyrs on the front. Cross Victoria Street at the lights and then the zebra crossing at Tothill Street. Carry on, walking down Storey's Gate. Cross straight over Birdcage Walk and walk all the way down Horse Guards Road. Note the tiny St James's Park police station. If you time it right and reach Horse Guards Parade for 11 a.m. (10 a.m. on Sundays), you will see the Queen's Guards and their horses gathering for the Changing of the Guard.

4. Cross the road at the impressive Guards' Memorial and go into St James's Park. Follow the path around the pond, passing the Inn at the Park café and keeping the pond on your left. Look out for the park's famous pelicans. At the blue bridge, turn right to leave the park through the gilded Marlborough Gates. Cross over the Mall and head down Marlborough Road. Note the lamps with crowns on them.

5. On your left is the red-brick, Tudor-style St James's Palace. This is another good spot to watch the Changing of the Guard, as the soldiers march by at the end of the ceremony, at around midday. You can't visit inside, but the Palace is steeped in history. Charles I spent his last night here before he was marched to Whitehall for his execution. It was the favourite palace of the first three King Georges, but Queen Victoria moved the

guard at Buckingham Palace

royal residence away from here to Buckingham Palace in 1837. St James's Palace is now used as royal offices and grace and favour apartments. You can attend services in the Queen's Chapel, designed by Inigo Jones, across the road. Walk past the palace and turn left on Pall Mall, passing the sentry boxes and the Chapel Royal, also open to the public for services. The heart and bowels of Mary I are buried here.

6. Walk down Cleveland Row, past Selwyn House and down the footpath into Green Park. Turn left towards the Mall, then walk towards the statue of Queen Victoria in front of Buckingham Palace. If the flag is flying, the Queen is at home. When you've peered through the railings at the sentries on duty, or visited the Palace (summers only), turn back and walk beside the gilded gates into Green Park, cutting diagonally right on a path towards the north-east corner, to Piccadilly by the Ritz hotel.

Guy Fawkes and the Gunpowder Plot

Remember, remember the fifth of November,
The gunpowder, treason and plot,
I know of no reason
Why the gunpowder treason
Should ever be forgot

Down in the cellars, back in 1605, Guy Fawkes and his friends laid barrels of gunpowder in an attempt to blow up Parliament and King James I. They were angry about the treatment of Catholics in England. Guy Fawkes was caught in the act and was duly tortured, hanged, drawn and quartered. His head was placed on a spike on London Bridge. That night, 5 November, bonfires were lit across England to celebrate the survival of the King. Bonfire Night has been celebrated every year since then, with effigies of Guy Fawkes traditionally burnt on a fire.

7. Turn left and hop on the tube at Green Park station. Or turn right to explore the smart streets of Piccadilly and have a well earned treat. If you've booked in advance, you can have tea at the Ritz. Otherwise, try out Fortnum and Mason, grocers to the Queen. Walk down Piccadilly and take a right on to St James's Street. Then turn left on Jermyn Street, and go in through the back door. Buy old-fashioned sweets from a jar, handmade chocolates, or freshly baked English cakes such as Eccles cakes, Bath buns, Battenberg cake and egg custard tarts to take home.

Eat me, drink me
There are plenty of cabins through St James's Park selling snacks and ice-creams, or you can eat a picnic in the park. For a special treat, book (well in advance) a royal tea at the Ritz, 50 Piccadilly, 020 7493 8181 www.theritzlondon.com.

Tea booking line 020 7300 2345. Weekend tea: book 4 months in advance; weekday tea: book 1 month in advance. (And check the dress code.) Or have an ice-cream sundae at the Parlour Restaurant in Fortnum and Mason, 181 Piccadilly. 020 7734 8040 www.fortnumandmason.com

Useful information

- Buckingham Palace Open daily, July to September. 020 7766 7300 www.royal.gov.uk
- Jewel Tower 020 7222 2219 www.english-heritage.org.uk
- Changing of the Guard takes place daily at 11 a.m. (10 a.m. on Sundays) at Horse Guards Parade and at 11.30 a.m. at Buckingham Palace, every day May to July, then on alternate days for the rest of the year. www.royal.gov.uk
- The Houses of Parliament Free advance tickets available from your local MP or Lord (UK residents only). Open to all in the summer holidays. Some tickets available on the day all year. 020 7219 3000 www.parliament.uk

Did you know?

- The Palace of Westminster, also known as the Houses of Parliament, has 1,100 rooms, 100 staircases and 3 miles of corridors.
- The number 2 on the clock at the entrance to Horse Guards Parade is marked with black to commemorate the hour of Charles I's execution.
- In the 1850s Queen Victoria requested Fortnum and Mason to send crates of its famous beef tea to Florence Nightingale in the Crimea for the soldiers.

11. Birdsong at Rainham Marshes

The Adventure

This trip takes us east along the Thames Estuary, heading out towards the sea. Still within sight of the City itself, this marshland landscape has remained unchanged for centuries. It was closed to the public for a hundred years when it was a Ministry of Defence site, but it has recently reopened as a Royal Society for the Protection of Birds (RSPB) nature reserve. Rifle ranges, ammunition stores and pillboxes, with some excellent war stories thrown in, provide an added attraction, but the main interest is the 250 or so different species of birds that visit this rare habitat.

Each season brings something different. Come spring, the air is filled with mating calls. In summer, young birds take their first flight and in autumn migrating birds move about in great numbers, either heading south to a warmer climate, or sheltering from the cold Arctic. In winter, large flocks of birds gather to feed, and at dusk fly around forming large roosts to keep warm. The marsh also supports small mammals, invertebrates, vertebrates and amphibians, including marsh frogs the size of tea plates, water voles, grass snakes, weasels and stoats. In the summer the reserve is a riot of colour, with banks of purple vetch and marsh thistles, yellow ox-tongue, sky-blue chicory and red poppies, and butterflies, dragonflies and damselflies proliferate. Become an ornithologist for the day, learning to identify birds through their markings and their birdsong. Keep a tally of what you see and note the day, date, time and location of the sighting. Most importantly, keep your eyes and ears open at all times so you don't miss anything. Remember to take your binoculars, or if you haven't any rent some at the Visitor Centre when you get there.

How far? 5.6 km/3½ miles
Start and finish Purfleet station

Walk the Walk

1. Get a mainline train from Fenchurch Street to Purfleet. Come out of Purfleet station, turn right and walk up London Road. It is a fifteen-minute walk to the marshes. Turn left at the Royal Hotel following the signs to Rainham Marshes. Turn right on to the riverside path. The river is very wide here: it holds more water as it nears the sea, as more tributaries have joined it along the way. At London Bridge the river is approximately 265m/870ft across, whereas on the coast at Whitstable where the Thames reaches the North Sea, it is 29 km/18 miles across.

    Just before crossing the brand new bridge, look closely down at the river near the bank. If the tide is out you will see some gigantic old black tree trunks. These have been preserved in the mud and are a mind-blowing six thousand

years old. Up ahead is the brightly coloured Visitor Centre. Keep walking towards it.

2. At the Visitor Centre you can hire a pair of binoculars (£2 per pair – it can pay to get a pair each, to avoid squabbling). Head out the back entrance of the building (you can see Canary Wharf on the horizon), walk down the ramp and take the Woodland Walk path, which is essentially a big loop which brings you back to the Visitor Centre at the end. Remember to keep your eyes and ears open all the time in case something flies or scuttles past. To get your ear in to the sound of the bird calls keep still, close your eyes and just listen to what is going on around you. There are many insects

hiding in the bulrushes, sought out by reed buntings, blue tits and even wrens, so you might hear them too.

3. At the Cordite Store take a left into a little wooded area and see what birds you can find. In the winter you have a chance of seeing a goldcrest, the UK's smallest songbird. Dull green on top and buff white below, it has a distinctive orange or yellow stripe on its crown. Come out at the opposite end from where you entered, on to a boardwalk. At the fork take a right to a feeding table nestled into the reeds. This provides a fantastic and almost guaranteed opportunity to see an array of birds. Get out your binoculars and make a start at studying markings. Stay here for a while – you won't often get an opportunity as good as this one. This is where having a pair of binoculars each can really pay off. Retrace your steps back to the fork and take what was originally the left-hand fork. You will pass a bog where you can see a 6,000-year-old piece of wood. If you notice any bumps on the ground while you are walking don't tread too hard on them, as they are probably the anthills of the yellow meadow ant.

4. You will now find yourself on a tarmac path. Near by there are some good hides. Pop in and have another session with your binoculars. When you look through the narrow viewing slits it's amazing how much suddenly comes into vision. Try and identify the birds: what colour are their wings/heads/legs? How long/what shape is its beak? Try drawing some of their distinguishing characteristics.

For instance: oystercatchers have bright orange beaks and red legs; curlews have long curved beaks; little egrets are all white with very long, thin, black beaks, black legs and yellow feet.

Keep going. You are now on the trail of a peregrine falcon – a large and powerful carnivorous bird, or raptor, that hunts and

WATER BIRDS

Black-tailed Godwit

Oystercatcher

Reed Bunting

Sand Martin

Wheatear

Whinchat

kills other animals. These birds are attracted by the wildfowl and waders here, especially in autumn and winter. Swift and agile in flight, a peregrine can be identified by blue-grey feathers on the upper body, a blackish top of the head and a black 'moustache' that contrasts with its white face. It has a short, stubby beak and its breast is finely spotted. Their nests, or eyries, are usually in inaccessible locations on cliff edges or in deserted buildings, so you're not that likely to see one today, although it's said that there is a breeding pair somewhere near here . . .

5. You will soon walk past Wennington Marsh where, during the war, buildings were specially erected for the sole purpose of burning them down. This was not as daft as it sounds: the burning buildings were decoys during the Blitz to trick the Luftwaffe into dropping their bombs here, in the middle of nowhere, instead of on the crowded streets of London.

Turn left on to the bridge, towards the disused target range, and think about having your picnic somewhere here. Look out for the many-coloured marsh frogs, ranging from bright green, through brown, to turquoise. On a warm, still day the frog chorus is deafening and sounds like bad belching. Grey herons, little egrets and grass snakes like to feed on them.

6. You might also spot a kestrel, which you can identify by its pointed wings and long tail and by its tendency to hover in the air. The hundred-year-old pillbox you can see is where the soldiers used to watch out for submarines coming up the Thames. It would have had guns mounted on top to shoot down Zeppelin planes.

You are now coming up to the recently opened Education Centre. In among the reeds you might well spy one or two of the ever-increasing numbers of water voles.

Marsh frog

7. Walk back up to the Visitor Centre to return your binoculars and then begin the walk back to Purfleet station.

Birdsong

A good way to help identify birds is by listening to and learning their call. Some have very distinctive sounds – the obvious one is a duck's 'quack'. Here are the sounds of some of the birds you might see or hear at Rainham.

Avocet: klute

Kestrel: kee-kee-kee

Kittiwake: kitti-way-ake

Lapwing: peewit

Osprey: tchip tchip tichip

Oystercatcher: kleep

Peregrine: kek-kek-kek

Skylark: chirrup

Eat me, drink me

Bring your own picnic (there are no shops) or eat at the café at Rainham Marshes.

Useful information

- For train times contact National Rail Enquiries 08457 48 49 50 www.nationalrail.co.uk
- For more information about Rainham Marshes 01708 899 840 www.rspb.org.uk

Books to read

Two stories about children befriending injured birds:
- *The Snow Goose* by Paul Gallico
- *A Kestrel for a Knave* by Barry Hines

Did you know?

- In medieval England, the only bird a knave was legally allowed to keep was a kestrel.
- The RSPB was formed to counter the trade in feathers from egrets and birds of paradise used in women's hats, which became fashionable in Victorian times.

12. On the Waterfront: Dockside London

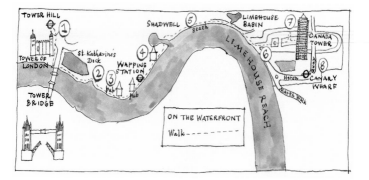

The Adventure

The stretch of the Thames from London Bridge to the Docks is known as the Pool of London. The expansion of London eastwards beyond Tower Bridge is relatively recent in terms of the city's history. It was only from the 1700s that wharfs, shipyards, cooperages, taverns, chandlers' shops, rope works and lodging houses sprang up. The heyday of the docks was in the eighteenth and nineteenth centuries when the area was crowded with people: dock workers loading and unloading exotic cargoes; lightermen and watermen working on the river; and the less desirable smugglers and pirates. It was also the centre of the slave trade: over three thousand ships left from London and carried nearly a million Africans into slavery, until the Abolition of the Slave Trade Act was passed in 1807.

Its days as a working dock ended in the 1960s, but many of the old buildings have been restored, providing an atmospheric journey. The street names are colourful as well as informative: Shoulder of Mutton Alley; Brewery Lane; Marble Quay; Gun Wharf. Pleasure boats have replaced the working boats and the skyscrapers of Canary Wharf tower over the scene. Take a picnic to eat on the beach, a bag for any mudlarking treasures you may find, and enjoy this journey through time.

How far? 8 km/5 miles
Start Tower Hill tube **Finish** Canary Wharf tube

Walk the Walk

1. Exit the tube station and walk down the steps, following the signs to the Tower of London. Turn left and walk alongside the Tower to the subway signposted to St Katharine's Dock, taking you under Tower Bridge Road. Turn right at the end and left into St Katharine's Dock, the centre of the Port of London. It was built by the Scottish engineer Thomas Telford in 1827–8. Ivory, sugar, shells, marble, wine, spices and perfumes were still being brought here up the river as recently as the 1930s. Walk straight on beside the boats and turn right just before Ivory House. Walk through the archway at the end and turn left. You will see Dickens Inn, a former spice warehouse reinvented as part of the 1980s regeneration of the area. Cross over the footbridge on your right.

2. At Marble Quay turn left, going straight down St Katharine's Way. At this point look out for signs to the Thames Path – it's a fair distance down, just after a narrow alley, the Alderman's Stairs, and before the clearly labelled Tower Bridge Wharf. You

The Canada
(Canary Wharf)

are now at the river's edge, opposite Butler's Wharf, which reputedly at one time contained the largest tea warehouse in the world. This is a good point to look back to get a great view of the iconic Tower Bridge.

3. From here on you are following the Thames Path signs, dipping in and out of the river's edge through Hermitage Memorial Gardens and scores of riverside flats until you are forced left to Wapping High Street. Turn right past the Georgian square of Wapping Pierhead. Take a look at the river at Wapping Old Stairs by the Town of Ramsgate pub. At one time there

were a staggering 140 pubs along here, many notorious as the haunts of pirates and smugglers. This one has been around since 1758. It was at Wapping Old Stairs that Judge Jeffreys, known as the Hanging Judge, was captured while trying to flee the country, disguised as a sailor, after the 1688 Glorious Revolution and James II's flight to France. He was put in the Tower for his own protection, but died there the following year. Walk down the lane by the pub for a beautiful view of the river. Retrace your steps to Wapping High Street and carry on.

At Wapping New Stairs cut down to the water's edge and look across the river to Rotherhithe, where Christopher Jones, captain of the *Mayflower*, lived. From here the ship set sail in 1620 for Southampton, where she picked up the Pilgrim Fathers for their voyage to America. Aside from the 102 passengers, the ship carried provisions including seeds, pigs, goats and chickens, and even a cooper to maintain the beer barrels. After a gruelling 66-day journey, the ship dropped anchor in Plymouth, Virginia.

Walk back to the road and keep going past the Marine Police Headquarters. There has been a marine police office in this area since 1798. Police were essential to curb the pilfering of cargo as the ships were being unloaded. Cargo was transferred direct from ships to 'lighters', or barges, handled by lightermen, while watermen were employed to row people, goods and equipment around the port. Both lightermen and watermen still work on the river today; they have an annual race from London Bridge to Chelsea Bridge.

4. Up ahead is the Captain Kidd Inn, so called after a notorious pirate sentenced to death in 1701. At nearby Execution Dock a permanent gibbet was set up at the low water mark and pirates would be hanged there until three tides had washed over them. Keep walking past the wharves. After Wapping tube station turn right through a gateway, following the Thames Path sign, to the widening river, then through another gate at St Hilda's Wharf. Take the steps on the right to the beach littered with oyster shells, bones, clay pipes, bits of broken china

Mudlarking

A mudlark is someone who scavenges at low tide in river mud for items of value. In past times mudlarks were usually young children who hoped to earn money by selling what they had found. Now mudlarking is more like being an amateur archaeologist. There are two ways of mudlarking. Either get a licence from the Port of London Authority (call 01474 562200 or see www.pla.co.uk) to be able to dig to a depth of 7.5cm/3in and to use a metal detector. Otherwise just riffle the surface with your fingers to see what you can find. There are usually loads of clay pipes right on the surface. If you do find something of potential merit take it to the Museum of London for identification and recording.

and lumps of chalk: a good place to mudlark. Walk back to Wapping High Street. Follow the Thames Path signs. Turn right at Wapping Wall and keep going all the way to Pelican Stairs and the Prospect of Whitby pub, which claims to be the oldest riverside inn, dating from around 1540. It was near here that the world's first underwater tunnel was built in 1825 by Sir Marc Brunel and his more famous son, Isambard.

5. Walk over the bridge at Shadwell Basin. Turn right following the Thames Path signs, and on through the King Edward Memorial Park. Follow the river path for a good stretch to Narrow Street. This area became a centre for world trade in Elizabethan times and by the reign of James I nearly half of the 2,000-strong population were mariners. Shipbuilding also throve here from the sixteenth to the nineteenth century.

At Limehouse, where the River Thames, the River Lea and the Regent's Canal all connect, cross over the marina bridge. This basin

A Wherry

is now used for river, canal and sea-going pleasure boats. Limehouse was London's original Chinatown, as large numbers of Chinese seamen and traders lived and worked here in the nineteenth century. Chinatown relocated to Soho after the devastation of the area in World War II. Turn right, back to the river, and keep going.

6. After Molines Wharf follow the sign to the river and cross over the pedestrian bridge. Carry on to Canary Wharf Pier. Once there turn left up the steps towards Canada Tower. Walk through the garden and keep going straight ahead.

7. Turn left down Willoughby Passage. Press the button in the wall to open the gate to West India Dock and the Museum of London Docklands in an old sugar warehouse. Ships sailed from the West India Dock, once the largest dock complex in the world, to West Africa, where they bought enslaved Africans

and took them to the Caribbean. After the human cargo had been sold the same ships loaded up with sugar and returned to London. It is recorded that 24,962 African slaves were taken to the Americas by ships sailing out of this dock.

8. Retrace your steps to Willoughby Passage and turn left to Canada Tower, which at 237m/778ft, topped by a pyramid, is one of the tallest buildings in England. From the station beneath you can take a ride on the space-age Docklands Light Railway. Or catch a Thames Clipper, departing every twenty minutes, from Canary Wharf Pier to Waterloo.

Eat me, drink me

Walk down Wapping High Street for Gordon Ramsay's The Narrow, www.gordonramsay.com/thenarrow. Or the Docklands Museum café is nice. A picnic on the beach is always something special.

Useful information

- Tower Bridge 020 7403 3761 www.towerbridge.org.uk
- St Katharine's Dock www.skdocks.co.uk
- Museum of London Docklands 020 7001 9844 www.museumindocklands.org.uk

Books to read

- *The Copper Treasure* by Melvin Burgess
- *Moonfleet* by John Meade Falkner

Did you know?

- In the 1700s a quarter of Britain's income came from imports from the West Indies.
- Canary Wharf is so called because at the west end of South Quay fresh fruit from the Canary Islands was unloaded into smaller barges.

cormorant

13. The Festival of Britain: Modern Art and Architecture

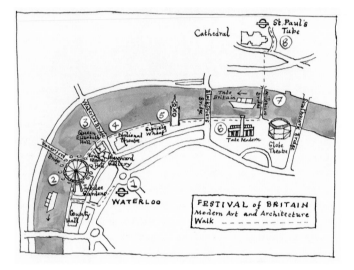

The Adventure

Post World War II was a period of austerity and rationing. Waterloo and the South Bank was a bombsite. When the Festival of Britain opened here on 3 May 1951, celebrating the centenary of the Great Exhibition, it provided a much-needed boost to morale and heralded the start of a new modern age. Works by modern artists such as Henry Moore and Barbara Hepworth were exhibited and the Festival Hall, the first modernist building in London, was built.

Everyone came to visit London and flocked to the South Bank with its new Dome of Discovery and the Skylon Tower. Today, the South Bank continues to be a place of entertainment, of innovative architecture, a centre for the arts and a site of national celebrations. The London Eye truly radiates the spirit of the 1951

Festival as well as being one of the most thrilling new additions to the London skyline. The riverside walkway and public spaces, first established in 1951, have been extended and on a sunny day the South Bank still enjoys a feeling of festival, with throngs of people being entertained by street performers.

How far? 3.2 km/2 miles
Start Waterloo tube **Finish** St Paul's or Pimlico tube

Walk the Walk

1. Come out of exit 6 on to York Road. Turn right and take the first right down Chicheley Street to Jubilee Gardens, created to mark the Queen's Silver Jubilee in 1977, on the site of the 1951 Festival. The avenue of plane trees commemorates London civilians who died in the war.

2. Head for the London Eye (architects Marks Barfield), built to celebrate the millennium, and at a height of 135m/443ft high the biggest Ferris wheel in Europe. This spot was the heart of the 1951 Festival, where the Dome of Discovery (architect Ralph Tubbs) stood. At 28m/93ft tall and 8m/26ft wide, this was once the largest dome in the world (the Millennium Dome is now biggest). It was divided into galleries: the Living World, Polar, the Sea, the Earth, the Physical World, the Land, Sky and Outer Space. It was later demolished and sold for scrap.

    Another temporary but trail-blazing structure was built here too: the 76m/250ft

Skylon (architects Powell & Moya). Rocket-like in shape, and appeared to float in the air as it was only anchored to the ground by a net of cables. Lit up at night by searchlights, it was a startlingly bright contrast to the blackout that had so recently shrouded London. Demolished in 1952, it was made into saucepans and ashtrays. There is now a campaign to rebuild it. Walk through the gardens, keeping the Thames on your left, and you will soon come to the first of the Southbank Centre buildings, all part of the legacy from the 1951 Festival. Firstly, the flagship permanent building: the Festival Hall (architects Leslie Martin, Peter Moro and Robert Matthew), which set the standard for new building design and the regeneration of bombed Britain. *Billy Budd*, an opera specially composed by Benjamin Britten, was performed here in celebration of the Festival.

3. Keep walking along the river's edge, under Hungerford Bridge, where, during the Festival, an additional temporary Bailey bridge was constructed to cope with the crowds: eight million visitors flocked to the South Bank between May and September 1951. You will soon come to the Queen Elizabeth Hall and Purcell Rooms (architects Hubert Bennett, Jack Whittle, F.G. West and Geoffrey Horsefall), officially opened in 1967. Tucked behind is the Hayward Gallery, distinctive for its Brutalist architecture typified by block geometric forms punched through with other geometric shapes and made from 'shutter boarded' concrete (a process where concrete is poured into a built

The Skylon

structure). Pop up to the Hayward, via the first level external balcony of the Queen Elizabeth Hall, and examine the texture, colour and feel of the building. Try to keep this in mind to compare with the concrete of the National Theatre – you will be surprised how different they are. The inside walls of the Gallery have the same finish as the outside, which is typical of the Brutalist style.

4. Walk back to the river's edge. There are lots of street performers here and it's a good spot for skateboarding. Head for Waterloo Bridge, another postwar build by Sir Giles Gilbert Scott (who also designed the iconic red telephone box). Walk under the bridge to the National Film Theatre where you can watch a free film from the national archive, including a documentary about the Festival of Britain, in the BFI Mediatheque.

The National Theatre, an archetype of Brutalist style, is just ahead. Architect Denys Lasdun took inspiration from its riverside location and designed it to look like a boat. The outside staircase acts as an anchor to the building. Look up at the 'prow of the ship'. Get up close and see how with its subtle wood grain pattern, smooth feel and grey colour it is quite different from the surface of the Hayward Gallery. This point in the river has a panorama that stretches from St Paul's Cathedral to Somerset House and on to Hawksmoor's towers at Westminster Abbey. Look out for the Barbican Tower, part of a Brutalist scheme in the City, rising above the dome of St Paul's.

5. Keep walking along the river, passing the London Television Centre and Gabriel's Wharf, a paved street with artisan shops, galleries and cafés. Continue along Queen's Walk to

Festival Pier, where you can climb down to a small beach to skim a stone or have a quick mudlark (see page 97). You are now at the Oxo Tower, a former power station, owned by the stock cube company, who, when denied planning permission to advertise on the tower, created windows which were 'coincidentally' in the shape of a circle, a cross and a circle. The tower is now full of artisan workshops and has a restaurant at the top with enviable river views.

6. Walk under Blackfriars Bridge towards another bastion of urban regeneration: Tate Modern. Originally a power station (designed by Sir Giles Gilbert Scott), it was rescued from demolition by the Twentieth Century Society and turned into this splendid gallery. The coloured light feature capping the towering chimney is by artist Michael Craig-Martin and at night it lights up the skyline, just as the Skylon Tower did in 1951.

7. To see the work of British artists featured in the 1951 Festival, hop on the Tate to Tate boat to Tate Britain. Then take the tube home from Pimlico. Alternatively, run over the Millennium Footbridge to St Paul's and the tube beyond.

The London Blitz

On 7 September 1940 London was attacked by 348 bombers and 617 fighter planes. 448 people were killed. The bombing continued for 76 nights. Many East Londoners camped overnight in Epping Forest; others used Anderson and Morrison shelters and some tube stations. The worst night of the Blitz was the last, when 3,000 people were killed. By the end of the Blitz on 11 May 1941, 20,000 Londoners had lost their lives, 1,400,000 were homeless and a million houses were destroyed or damaged. Even Buckingham Palace had been bombed. Boy Scouts and Girl Guides helped by guiding fire engines to bombsites.

Eat me, drink me

There are plenty of cafés and restaurants all along the South Bank.

Useful information

- The South Bank Centre, including the Hayward Gallery, Queen Elizabeth Hall and Royal Festival Hall
  020 7960 4200 www.southbankcentre.co.uk
- National Theatre box office
  020 7452 3000 www.nationaltheatre.org.uk.
- Tate Modern and Tate Britain
  020 7887 8888 www.tate.org.uk.

Further afield

- The Twentieth Century Society safeguards architecture and design dating from 1914 onwards.
  020 7250 3857 www.c20society.org.uk
- The Design Museum specializes in twentieth-century design.
  020 7403 6933 www.designmuseum.org
- Visit the Blitz Experience at the Imperial War Museum.
  020 7416 5320 www.londoniwm.org.uk

Books to read

Two books about children in wartime Britain:
- *Carrie's War* by Nina Bawden
- *Friend or Foe* by Michael Morpurgo

Did you know?

- In 1951 Charles Elleano walked across the Thames on a tight rope.
- As part of the 1951 Festival of Britain, Battersea Park was turned into an amusement park with a big dipper, a boating lake, a tree-walk, a miniature railway and fantastic fountains.

14. Street Life: London's coolest Markets

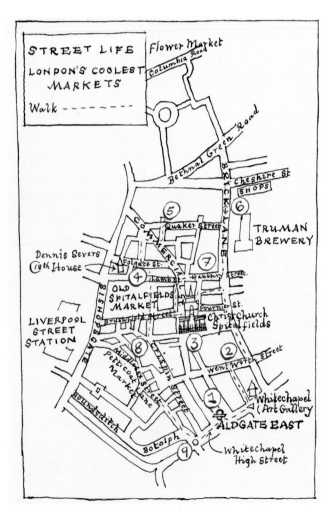

The Adventure

The bustle of Spitalfields and Brick Lane is rich with the cultural history of London. Jewish bagel bakeries, Indian curry houses, artists and artisan shops and hip markets make it one of the most exciting parts of London. Old Spitalfields has been turned into a covered market for records, clothes, music and food. Brick Lane has one of London's best street markets and on Sundays Columbia Road, to the north, is London's great flower market. The area is home to London's artists, with Tracey Emin and Gilbert and George living here, the Whitechapel Art Gallery at the end of Brick Lane and the art galleries of Hoxton nearby.

It has always been a place for immigrants new to London, just outside the walls of the old city. Many of the streets are characterized by the elegant Georgian houses built by the French Huguenots, Protestants who came to live here when they were forced out of Catholic France. Many of them were silk weavers. They built large, simple, shuttered houses with vast attic spaces for working the silk looms. As they became wealthy, they moved away, making way for the next generation of immigrants to Spitalfields. The Huguenots were followed by Irish weavers, and, in turn, by Ashkenazi Jews, escaping from Russian persecution in the late nineteenth and early twentieth centuries. Most recently, people from Bangladesh settled here in the mid-twentieth century. Spitalfields is now a thriving, regenerated part of London.

How far? 4 km/2½ miles
Start and finish Aldgate East tube

Walk the Walk

1. Leave by exit 3. Turn right past the Whitechapel Art Gallery and then right again through an arch between the shops, into Gunthorpe Street.
2. Turn right on to Wentworth Street, then left into Brick Lane. This

street has the highest density of Indian restaurants in England, but was once more famous for its silk weavers and shops.

As you walk up Brick Lane, look out for the mosque on the corner of Fournier Street. This little building captures the history of these streets. It began life in 1742 as La Neuve Eglise, a Huguenot chapel. By 1809 it was known as the Jews' Chapel, built to promote Christianity to Jews. By 1898 it had become the Spitalfields Great Synagogue. Finally, in 1976 it became a mosque, the London Jamme Masjid. Turn left into Princelet Street and admire the best preserved Huguenot houses in London, with their beautiful painted wooden shutters in reds, purples and greys, several still forlorn and neglected with peeling paint and faded colours, others rescued and restored. Note the shutters are, in French style, on the outside of the houses. No. 19 houses the Museum of Immigration and Diversity, with a hidden synagogue dating from 1869. You can stay at No. 13 through the Landmark Trust (www.landmarktrust.org.uk).

3. Turn left into Wilkes Street, looking out for Banksy-style graffiti on the way. Then turn right into Fournier Street, towards Spitalfields Market and the impressive spired Hawksmoor Christ Church. Built by Queen Anne for the 'godless thousands' of the East End between 1714 and 1729, the church is worth stopping in for a few moments if only to admire its grandeur. Virtually derelict in 1960, it has recently been beautifully restored.

Leaving the church down the steps, cross the road and walk down the side of the market on Brushfield Street. Cross Crispin Street and pass a row of tempting cafés, pausing at the last, A. Gold, to buy sweets from a jar (sugar mice, fudge, liquorice, sherbert fountains) or have a coffee in the cramped, charming shop surrounded by delicious jams, elderflower wines, fresh

church

bread, and seven-day marmalade. The café is owned by the writer Jeanette Winterson. Cross to the other side of Brushfield Street and explore the market as much as you like (stalls open Monday to Friday and Sundays). Leave on the opposite side. Turn left on Lamb Street, then right on to Spital Square.

4. Turn left down Folgate Street and walk to No.18, Dennis Severs' extraordinary restoration of a Huguenot weaver's house, authentic to the last detail. Note the gas lamp burning outside, peer through the windows for a taste of the atmosphere inside. If you have older children it is worth timing your visit so you can see inside this wonderful house.

    Look up at the contrast of the Georgian street with the City towers behind it before turning right on to Blossom Street, passing old warehouses and bending right to Fleur de Lis Street. At the end of the street, cross Commercial Street and turn left down Wheler Street.

5. Turn right down Quaker Street. Continue to Brick Lane and then turn left. The famous Truman Brewery chimney dominates

this part of the street. Back in 1683, Joseph Truman established the great Black Eagle Brewery here on Brick Lane, drawing water from deep wells beneath it.

6. Walk up Brick Lane, under the railway bridge. If you fancy taking a detour turn right into Cheshire Street to explore the unusual, arty and trendy smattering of shops, with vintage clothing, t-shirts, interiors, children's clothes and toys. There is a tat market here on Sundays, with clothes and junk for sale.

   Turn left back down Brick Lane, heading past the Brewery (now the site of two hip and trendy markets). Stop for a curry at one of the many Bangladeshi restaurants.

7. Turn right down Hanbury Street, cross back over Commercial Street and turn left then right into Brushfield Street. Then take the first left down Crispin Street. Turn right down Artillery Lane and feed left down the alleyway called Artillery Passage.

8. Turn left down Sandys Row at the King's Stores pub, then left on to Middlesex Street, otherwise known as Petticoat Lane, where there is a street market selling end of season fashions, on every day except Saturday.

Street Talk

In the late nineteenth century, thousands of Jewish people fled the terror of pogroms in eastern Europe and came to London. Lots of the Yiddish words they used have become part of everyday English.

Chutzpah guts and daring
Glitch a slip or error
Nebbish a fool, a nobody
Schlep to drag or have a tedious journey
Schmaltz over-sentimental
Schmooze make small talk, be sociable

9. At the end of the street, turn left on to Botolph Street. Follow it left as it becomes Whitechapel High Street and leads back to the tube station at Aldgate East.

Eat me, drink me

Brick Lane is famed for its exceptional and spicy curries, or pick up some fresh bagels, a legacy of its Jewish past. Inside Spitalfields market there are stalls that cook fresh Asian food.

Useful information

- The Brick Lane flea market is open on Sundays 8 a.m. to 2 p.m.
- In both the Backyard Market (Saturdays and Sundays) and the UpMarket (Sundays only) at the Old Truman Brewery you will find young artists and designers selling fashion, crafts and music. www.trumanbrewery.com
- Spitalfields market shops and restaurants are open all week, but there are no market stalls on Saturdays. www.spitalfields.co.uk
- Petticoat Lane market on Middlesex Street is open Monday to Friday 9 a.m. to 2 p.m. and Sunday mornings.

- Whitechapel Art Gallery 020 7522 7888
  www.whitechapelgallery.org
- Dennis Severs' House is open every first and third Sunday
  12 a.m. to 4 p.m. without booking. Check the website for
  opening times. Not suitable for very young children.
  020 7247 4013 www.dennissevershouse.co.uk
- Museum of Immigration and Diversity. 020 7247 5352
  www.19princeletstreet.org.uk

Further afield
- Columbia Road Flower Market. Just ten minutes north of Brick
  Lane, this is one of London's loveliest markets for plants and
  fresh flowers. Open Sunday mornings 8 a.m. to 2 p.m.
  www.columbia-flower-market.freewebspace.com
- V&A Museum of Childhood, Cambridge Heath Road,
  London E2 9PA. Not too far away is this excellent and free
  museum with changing exhibitions and permanent displays of
  children's toys, games and nursery rhymes.
  020 8983 5200 www.vam.ac.uk

Books to read
- *The Tiger in the Well* by Philip Pullman. One of the Sally
  Lockhart quartet, partly set in nineteenth-century Jewish
  Spitalfields
- *Smith* by Leon Garfield. An atmospheric foggy London
  adventure set in the city

Did you know?
- Spitalfields lies just outside the old
  City walls. It is where the dead were
  buried and dead dogs were thrown
  (Houndsditch).
- All of Jack the Ripper's victims lived in
  Spitalfields. Two were murdered here.

Pigeon

15. Dick Whittington and the City of London

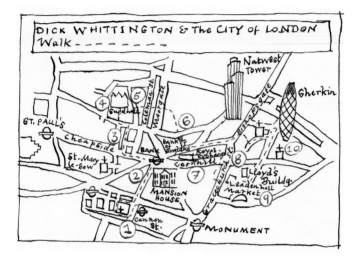

The Adventure

Sir Richard Whittington was Lord Mayor of London four times between 1397 and 1420, a time when Westminster and the City of London had separate governments and the Lord Mayor rivalled the monarch for power. Whittington came to London to join the City Guild of Mercers as an apprentice. The Guild of Mercers was one of the institutions that have helped to make the City of London the centre of finance it is today, and Whittington became extremely wealthy. In his time the City, which was just over a square mile (hence the nickname), was encircled by a wall which still defines its boundaries today. Packed into this confined space are all the key City offices: the Guildhall, the Mansion House, the Bank of England, the Lloyds Building and the Livery Company Halls.

Dick Whittington's cat

Uncover hidden alleys, decipher street names and develop an understanding of what the medieval City was like in Dick Whittington's day. Discover the tallest buildings, the oldest buildings, the funniest-shaped buildings and buildings that haven't even been built yet. The City of London is the oldest continuous municipal democracy in the world. Find out what makes it tick.

How far? 3.2 km/2 miles
Start Cannon Street tube **Finish** Bank tube

Walk the Walk

1. Take the Dowgate Hill exit from the tube and turn left, then turn right at College Street and walk to the corner of College Hill and into St Michael Paternoster Royal, a church built with Whittington's money and the place where he was buried. There is a stained glass window and a plaque in the floor by the altar dedicated to him. He lived in a house next door.

2. Turn right up College Hill, then right into Cloak Lane and back to Dowgate Hill, where you turn left and cross over Cannon Street. Head up Walbrook to the Mansion House, the Palladian-style Georgian town palace and official residence of the Lord Mayor since 1752 (tours Tuesdays at 2 p.m., or just peek into the Great Hall). The Lord Mayor is elected for one year only; the position is unpaid and apolitical. The best way to see the Lord Mayor is at the annual parade of the Lord Mayor's Show, where he processes through the City in his golden coach.

3. Cross Queen Victoria Street. Turn left down Poultry, past Grocers' Hall, the home of one of the City's 108 livery companies or guilds, developed in medieval times to protect the interests of groups of merchants and tradesmen. They have provided the foundation of much of the City's wealth. You will soon be on

Cheapside, the site of the main produce market in medieval London: 'cheap' loosely meaning 'market' in medieval English. The street names can tell us what was traded here: Poultry, Honey Lane, Milk Street and Bread Street.

Watch out for Ironmonger Lane on your right. Stop just here and listen for the sound of Bow Bells ringing from the nearby church of St Mary-le-Bow. It is a key part of London folklore that if you are born within the sound of Bow Bells you are a true Londoner or cockney. In the fable of Dick Whittington's life it was these bells which stopped him leaving London as he thought he heard them sing to him: 'Turn again, turn again, Lord Mayor of London'.

4. Turn right down Ironmonger Lane, home to Dick Whittington's guild, the Worshipful Company of Mercers, incorporated

under a royal charter in 1394. The Mercers, who dealt in fine fabrics, rank first among the livery companies of the City. The first Mercers' Hall was burnt down in the Great Fire (see pages 17–24), the second destroyed during the Blitz (see page 104). Look out for the current Hall on the right.

5. At the bottom of the road turn left into Gresham Street and shortly on your right, set back, is the gleaming pale stone of the Guildhall, a city powerhouse since the twelfth century, now the base of the Corporation of London. Find the stained glass window of Dick Whittington in the Great Hall and the listings, in the window recesses, of all the seven hundred or so Lord Mayors since 1189. The banners hanging on high represent the twelve Great Livery Companies of London. Dick Whittington entertained Henry V here and the Lord Mayor's Banquet is still held here every year. Outside, look for the statue of Dick Whittington and his cat near the Guildhall Art Gallery, where you can see a painting of the Lord Mayor and the remains of a fabulous Roman amphitheatre.

Turn left down the side of the gallery on Guildhall Buildings, past the Lord Mayor's law courts and left into Basinghall Street. Then turn right into Mason's Avenue and out on to Coleman Street. The Armourers' Hall is at the bottom on the right. Look left to see the startlingly modern Austral Building, built in 2006 and reminiscent of a honeycomb.

The Gherkin

6. Cross straight over to Great Bell Alley and be bowled over by the view of Tower 42 (formally the NatWest Tower), built in 1980 and in 2009 still the tallest building in the square mile and the sixth-tallest building in London. Cross Moorgate and keep going down Telegraph Street. Look out for an old-fashioned barber shop sign – there is a small passageway just here on the right that will take you to Tokenhouse Yard. At the end, turn left on Lothbury and then right into

Bartholomew Lane. You are now at the Bank of England, the United Kingdom's central bank, nicknamed the Old Lady of Threadneedle Street. Its first home was in the Mercers' Hall but it has been on this site since 1734. In the museum you can learn all about money and currencies and

Arms of dick Whittington

even handle a solid gold bar. Author Kenneth Grahame was working in the Bank when he wrote *Wind in the Willows*.

7. Cross Threadneedle Street, which got its name from the siting of the Merchant Taylors' Livery Company at No. 30. Turn right to walk around to the front of the Corinthian-columned Royal Exchange, holding forth in the middle of the square and created in 1565 by London merchant Sir Thomas Gresham, as a place for merchants and tradesmen to meet and do business. It no longer serves its original function but walk through it and on the galleried level take a look at the wall paintings depicting the history of the Royal Exchange and the City. Exit at the far left corner, past a bust of President Lincoln and, just outside, a bust of Paul Julius Reuter, founder of Reuters news agency.

8. Turn left into Royal Exchange Buildings, and then right into Royal Exchange Avenue (just before Threadneedle Street) and right again on to Finch Lane. Cross over Cornhill and into an alley, Ball Court, past the old Simpson's Tavern, which has been on this site since 1757; it was two houses, then became a chophouse and coffee shop. Turn left into Castle Court past another historic inn, the George and Vulture, here since 1600: Dickens mentions it many times and when it was threatened with demolition the author's great-grandson saved it. Do pop in for a look. Keep going straight ahead, then turn right into Bell Inn Yard and left on to Gracechurch Street.

Cross over and head left. Turn right into Leadenhall Market, a focal point of the City since Roman times. Dick Whittington

bought this site in 1411 and it steadily grew in importance: in 1463 the beam for the weighing of wool was fixed here; in 1488 this was the only place allowed to trade in leather; and in 1622 the same applied to cutlery. Rebuilt after the Great Fire, it became a covered market and was divided into the beef market, the green yard and the herb market.

9. Walk straight out the other end of Leadenhall Market; you will think you have walked through a time machine and been blasted straight into the twenty-first century. The ultra-modern Lloyds building is slap bang on the left. The Swiss Re building, the distinctive rocket-shaped tower at 30 St Mary Axe that is usually referred to as the Gherkin, looms ahead. Lloyds, the world's leading insurance market, was founded in 1688. The current building, designed by Richard Rogers, is known as the 'inside out building' because all the services, such as lifts, staircases and water pipes, are on the outside of the building to make a clutter-free space inside.

10. Walk through the passageway down Lime Street and over Leadenhall Street towards St Andrews Undershaft and the Gherkin, designed by Norman Foster. It is 180m/590ft high and (in 2009) the seventh-tallest structure in London. Look back for a great view of the Lloyds building.

Turn left down Undershaft (directly opposite the Gherkin) and walk towards Tower 42, past the fifteenth-century church of St Helen's Bishopsgate. When you are in front of the church, turn round for a great view of contrasts: the very old and very new. Turn left, out on to Bishopsgate, cross over at the lights (opposite Gibson's Hall) and walk down Threadneedle Street to Bank tube station.

Eat me, drink me

There are plenty of places to eat in the City during the week but fewer options at the weekend, so bring supplies.

Useful information

- The Guildhall 020 7606 3030 www.guildhall.cityoflondon.gov.uk
- Bank of England Museum 020 7601 5545 www.bankofengland.co.uk
- The Lord Mayor's Show www.lordmayorsshow.org
- Museum of London 020 7001 9844 www.museumoflondon.org.uk

Books to read

- *Ring out Bow Bells* by Cynthia Harnett. A gripping story about the life of an apprentice in medieval London.
- *Humbert, Mr Firking and The Lord Mayor of London* by John Burningham.

Did you know?

- The first performance of the pantomime *Dick Whittington* was in 1814 at Covent Garden.
- Whittington paid for the building of a 64-seater public lavatory (32 seats for women, 32 for men). It overhung the river and was known as Whittington's Longhouse.

16. coram Boy:
The story of a Georgian orphan

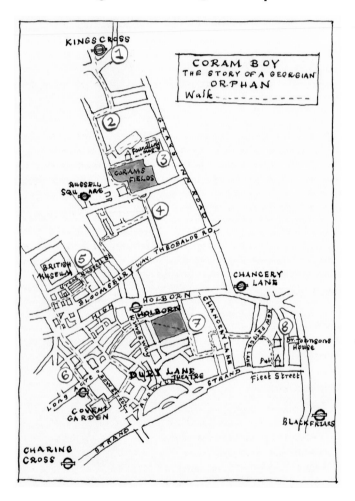

CORAM BOY
THE STORY OF A GEORGIAN
ORPHAN
Walk ------

The Adventure

Coram Boy is the story of two boys, Aaron and Toby, abandoned children of unknown parentage, or 'foundlings'. They lived at the Foundling Hospital, the first children's home in Britain, established by Thomas Coram in 1739. The book is set in early Georgian times when London was filled with the stench of wet horse poo, chamber pots were emptied out of windows, and dead dogs, cats, rats and even horses were left to rot in the streets. Society was divided between the rich and the very poor. The poor lived in unhealthy cramped conditions, or in workhouses, or on the street. Many children were abandoned by their desperate parents. A shocking 75 per cent of London children died before the age of five.

Visit Coram's Fields where foundling children lived, now one of London's loveliest playgrounds, run through the streets of Covent Garden as the boys in the story would have done, past the theatres and street performers, and visit a Georgian house just like the ones where the boys might have gone to work. Help bring the story alive with a copy of the book in hand and imagine yourself as a lamp light boy, carrying a flaming torch and showing gentlemen around the dirty, dark streets, many of which were still little more than muddy country lanes.

How far? 4 km/2½ miles
Start King's Cross tube
Finish Chancery Lane tube

Walk the Walk

1. Leave King's Cross by the Euston Road south side exit. Turn right up the stairs to Camden Town Hall and then left into Argyle Street. Turn right into Whidborne Street, right again at Cromer Street, then left into Judd Street.

2. Cross Tavistock Place and keep going on Hunter Street. Turn left into Handel Street and into St George's Gardens, a former burial ground, recognizable from *Coram Boy* as the place Aaron lay on a tombstone listening to music played in the Foundlings' chapel. Walk to the far end and leave by the right-hand gates.

3. Turn left down Heathcote Street, right into Mecklenburgh Street and right again at Mecklenburgh Square. Head through the gate by the Coram Foundation, immediately turning left to walk along a narrow passageway behind Coram's Fields. This children's playground is the site of the Foundling Hospital, demolished in the 1920s.

At the end, on the right, is the Foundling Museum, which tells the story of the place and its people. To be admitted, babies had to be healthy and under two months old. A lottery system operated where coloured balls were taken from a bag: white meant a place; red the reserves list; and black no place. Once children were five they were taught to read and write and expected to do chores. Boys were set to rope-making and outdoor jobs and girls did indoor work: sewing, spinning and cleaning, to prepare them to go out to work at twelve or thirteen. The Hospital was funded by patrons including the composer Handel and the artist Hogarth. The latter had the novel idea of asking artists to donate works which the public could then pay to view (there were no public art galleries at that time).  The collection contains work by Reynolds and Gainsborough, on view in the upstairs Georgian panelled rooms. Climb the oak staircase, the original from the boys' wing of the Hospital, and look at Hogarth's portrait of Captain Thomas Coram, the man that Aaron thought he was praying to when he said the Lord's Prayer at night.

Exit the museum and walk through the gardens in front of you to Lansdowne Terrace. The low white buildings on the other side of the railings are original to the Foundling Hospital. Turn left on Guilford Street and pop into Coram's Fields for a play. When you come out, cross over the zebra crossing to Guilford Place and up Lamb's Conduit Street, named after the man who built a conduit here to carry water to the city.

4. Turn right into Great Ormond Street and you will pass the Hospital for Children, founded in 1852, the first hospital for sick children in the English-speaking world. This too benefited from philanthropy: J.M. Barrie bequeathed the copyright of *Peter Pan* to the hospital.

5. Cross straight over Queen Square and take Cosmo Place to Southampton Row. Cross over and turn left and then right into Bloomsbury Place. Find the blue plaque dedicated to Sir Hans Sloane on one of the stucco-fronted houses. Physician, naturalist and collector, Sloane bequeathed his library,

herbarium and vast collection of objects to King George II for the nation. Together with the King's Old Royal Library and other donations this became the British Museum, which opened its doors in 1759 in Montagu House, on the site of the current museum building, which has its main entrance on Great Russell Street, just down the road from Sloane's house.

Opposite the Museum is Bury Place. Walk down here past the London Review Bookshop (and café), and the Stamp Company shop, where you can pick up a dipping pen, ink, sealing wax and seal for writing a letter in eighteenth-century style.

Turn right down Little Russell Street, past the back of St George's Bloomsbury, designed by Nicholas Hawksmoor. Cross Museum Street, popping into the Cartoon Museum to view an original Hogarth cartoon. Turn right at Coptic Street, left on to Streatham Street and left again on to Bloomsbury Street. Cross over New Oxford Street and head down Shaftesbury Avenue towards the Oasis Sports Centre.

6. Walk down Endell Street and take a right at Shelton Street. Turn left down Neal Street and cross Long Acre into James Street. Covent Garden Piazza is ahead – an 'experiment in town planning' which was until the 1700s still agricultural land. Designed by Inigo Jones, it was once the home of London's principal fruit, vegetable and flower market. It has long been a centre for theatre: Samuel Pepys noted in his

diary in 1662 that he saw his first Punch and Judy show here. In the eighteenth century the streets would have been heaving with street entertainers just as they are today.

At the bottom of James Street turn left to walk round the back of the Royal Opera House. In 1743, when it was known as the Covent Garden Theatre, Handel's *Messiah* had its first London performance here. Turn left down Russell Street and look for the plaque at Boswell's coffee house, commemorating the first meeting in 1763 of Dr Samuel Johnson, the man who wrote the first dictionary of the English language, and his biographer and 'constant observer' James Boswell. Johnson, although not a patron, visited the Foundling Hospital and gave a home to an ex-slave boy, treating him like a son.

Cross over Bow Street, home of the 'Bow Street runners', the first incarnation of the Metropolitan Police Force, established in 1749 by magistrate and author Henry Fielding. Carry on into Russell Street and walk under the colonnade of the Theatre Royal, Drury Lane, the oldest theatre in Covent Garden. Imagine you are Timothy, the boy Aaron worked with, rushing to catch a glimpse of Nancy Dawson, who regularly appeared here.

7. Turn left up Drury Lane and then right on to Great Queen Street. Walk up to Kingsway, cross over and go straight ahead down Remnant Street to Lincoln's Inn Fields – an ideal picnic spot. On the left is Sir John Soane's Museum, a late Georgian interior and collection preserved so far as possible as Soane left it. If you've had enough, go back to Kingsway and turn right to Holborn tube station.

8. Otherwise, for a real eighteenth-century treat, cut diagonally across Lincoln's Inn Fields, down Serle Street, left down Carey Street, left into Chancery Lane, right into Bream's Buildings and right again into Fetter Lane. Turn left at West Harding Street and continue to Pemberton Row. Turn right into Gough Square. In the

Recipe for Gruel

Gruel was the staple food of the Foundling Hospital. It was a watery soup made from oatmeal.

Ingredients
3 dessert spoons oatmeal • 1 pint water • pinch of salt

- Mix together the oatmeal and a little water to make a paste.
- Slowly add more water and boil for ten minutes, then add the salt. Serve with a severe face.

corner is Dr Johnson's House. Look around to see how he lived and where he worked and, if you like, dress up in the period costumes. You can see a copy of the first English dictionary upstairs in the room where Dr Johnson wrote it. One of his most famous sayings was 'When a man is tired of London, he is tired of life.' For a final stop, pop into his local, Ye Olde Cheshire Cheese pub in Wine Office Court. To get there head to the statue of Hodge, Johnson's cat, turn right and walk down towards Fleet Street. Travel home from Blackfriars (closed until late 2011) or Chancery Lane tube.

Eat me, drink me
There is a café at the Foundling Museum and Covent Garden offers many options. Coram's Fields and Lincoln's Inn Fields are good for picnics or try Ye Old Cheshire Cheese for a pub lunch.

Useful information
- The Foundling Museum 020 7841 3600
  www.foundlingmuseum.org.uk
- Dr Johnson's House, closed on Sundays
  020 7353 3745 www.drjohnsonshouse.org

An Old London Song to Sing

Oh, do you know the muffin man,
the muffin man, the muffin man,
Oh, do you know the muffin man,
who lives in Drury Lane?

Oh, yes, I know the muffin man,
The muffin man, the muffin man,
Oh, yes, I know the muffin man,
Who lives in Drury Lane.

- Sir John Soane's Museum 020 7405 2107 www.soane.org
- The British Museum 020 7323 8000
  www.britishmuseum.org
- Benjamin Pollock's Toyshop 0207 379 7866
  www.pollocks-coventgarden.co.uk.

Books to read
- *Coram Boy* by Jamila Gavin
- *Tom Jones* by Henry Fielding. An eighteenth-century comic
  novel with an orphan as hero.

Did you know?
- All babies at the Foundling Hospital were
  inoculated against smallpox – an innovative
  health care programme of the time.
- 18,539 children were admitted to the
  Foundling Hospital between 1741 and 1799.

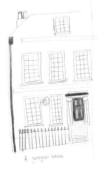

A georgian house

17. Peter Pan in Kensington Gardens

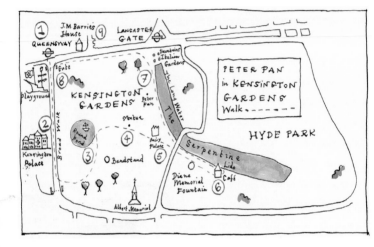

The Adventure

Explore Kensington Gardens with one of the most enchanting children's characters, Peter Pan, the boy who never grew up. The author, J.M. Barrie, lived just across the road and walked here daily with his St Bernard dog, Porthos. It was on one of these strolls, in 1897, that Barrie met two of the Llewellyn Davies brothers, George, aged four, and his brother Jack, aged three. This was the start of a life-long friendship and the inspiration for Barrie's stories. The admiration was mutual. To young George, Barrie seemed 'singularly well informed on the subject of cricket, fairies, murderers, pirates, hangings, desert islands and verbs that take the dative.'

Discover your own Neverland in a world of make-believe games at Kensington Gardens, the ideal place to let any lost boy's, pirate's, redskin's or fairy's imagination run wild. It provides any Peter Pan-ish children with 111 hectares/ 275 acres to run wild in and thousands of trees to hide behind. As well as your bows and arrows, a model boat, and a copy of *Peter Pan*, take along your swimming things because, in the summer, you can plunge into the Serpentine for a swim.

How far? 5.6 km/3½ miles
Start and finish Queensway tube

Walk the Walk

1. Exit Queensway station, cross over Bayswater Road and enter the park through Black Lion Gate. On the right is the Diana Princess of Wales Memorial playground (which we will visit later). Look out for the elfin oak, a gnarled and partially hollow stump, carved with fairies, elves and animals.

2. Stroll along the wide avenue of the Broad Walk, the main thoroughfare of the Gardens passing between Kensington Palace and the Round Pond. This is where, in the days when the Darling family were growing up, children would be pushed in perambulators by their nurses. The Darlings' nurse was a dog called Nana, whom they first met in Kensington Gardens. She was a Newfoundland whose character was based on Barrie's own dog. In the story of Peter Pan if you fell out of your perambulator and weren't claimed for seven days you would be sent to Neverland and become a Lost Boy. Peter Pan was the Lost Boys' Captain.

   On your right is Kensington Palace, which has been a royal residence since the seventeenth century. Queen Victoria was born in Kensington Palace and lived there until she moved to Buckingham Palace in 1837. It was Princess Diana's home from her marriage to Prince Charles in 1981 until she died in 1997. It is worth a look round, especially Queen Victoria's bedroom. In *Peter Pan in Kensington Gardens* the Queen of the Fairies lived here all alone with only lots of dolls for company. She was rather spoilt.

Continue along the Broad Walk, and down a gentle slope towards a mound. In the autumn, this is a good place to try and catch falling leaves. Alternatively, you could collect some leaves to take home and make a costume like the one Tinkerbell wore when she first visited the Darling children in their nursery, 'exquisitely gowned in a skeleton leaf'. You might need more than one leaf.

3. Before you reach Palace Gate, leading out on to Kensington Gore, take the penultimate path on the left along Flower Walk. Take the second left at the finger post, towards the Round Pond. Off to the left here is a good place to play cricket or a game of tag. Choose a character from the book, and run round chasing each other, just like they all did in Neverland, until you are thoroughly exhausted. Or pick up a stick, make a cutlass and have a fierce battle.

At the Round Pond, launch your model boat. If you don't have one, try an even better alternative recommended in *Peter Pan in Kensington Gardens*: 'the sweetest craft that slips her moorings in the Round Pond is what is called a stick-boat, because she is rather like a stick until she is in the water and you are holding the string.' Do be careful not to fall in – there won't be any ticking crocodiles but you might meet a three-spined stickleback, a roach, a gudgeon or some eels.

A Crocodile

4. Walk away from the pond with Kensington Palace behind you and the horse and rider, the statue of Physical Energy, directly in front. The grass here has been

allowed to grow long to improve the habitat for birds, bees and wild flowers, which you can expect to see in the spring and summer. This is also a good spot for a picnic and some storytelling. Peter Pan was very fond of stories, particularly stories about himself. It was Wendy's boast that she had some good stories to tell the Lost Boys that made Peter decide to take the Darling children with him to Neverland. Why don't you make a miniature Wendy house with sticks, grass and leaves?

5. At the six-way junction by the statue, look over to your right and you will see in the distance the gleaming golden splendour of the Albert Memorial, built to commemorate Queen Victoria's beloved husband. From here, with the Long Water ahead, make your own path through the trees in the direction of Queen Caroline's Temple. Walk past it towards a tarmac path which

clings to the side of the water. When you reach it turn right and walk under the Serpentine Bridge towards the Princess of Wales Memorial Fountain and the Lido, venue for the 2012 Olympic triathlon and open water swimming events and your chance for a swim. In the summer, when the pool is open to the public, the average temperature is 20°C. For the annual Peter Pan Christmas Day Race, for which J.M. Barrie donated a cup, it is probably freezing. You are now officially in Hyde Park, the site of several national celebrations including the 1851 Great Exhibition and in 1977 the Queen's Silver Jubilee Exhibition.

6. Stop at the Lido Café for a juice and a biscuit. The lake was created in 1728 by Queen Caroline, wife of George II, who was also responsible for creating Kensington Gardens, which were opened, on Saturdays only, to the public (you had to be 'respectably dressed'). The most important thing to look for is the island far away up the lake to the right, probably the inspiration for Neverland, where Peter Pan takes Wendy, John and Michael once they have learned to fly. Can you see any

Make an Indian Headdress

While you are in the park collect as many feathers and leaves as you can. Take them home. Measure your head with a piece of string. Cut out a band of brown paper 7cm/3in wide and twice as long as the size of your head plus another 12.5cm/5in. Fold the piece of paper in half lengthways, and lay it on a table. This would be a good moment to draw on a pattern with some colouring pens. Otherwise, just lay out the leaves and feathers, popping them inside the folded paper, with the tallest ones in the middle. Keep laying out your feathers and leaves until you get 6.5cm/2 ½in away from each end. Then staple or glue them on to the head band. Staple the two ends of the head band together. If you want to make it more Hiawatha than Indian Chief you could always add some ribbons.

smoke from the redskins' bonfire on the horizon?

In the real world, this island is a bird sanctuary: some unusual species have been spotted. Do report any unusual sightings to the park-keeper, as bird records for Kensington Gardens go back more than a hundred years. The lake also attracts a large number of insects that provide a perfect feeding ground for bats, which you can see at dusk.

7. Turn round, head back under the bridge and walk along the edge of Long Water until you reach the bronze Peter Pan statue on the left. This was meant to be modelled on Michael Llewelyn Davies but the sculptor chose another child and Barrie was quite unhappy about it.

8. Walk towards the Italianate gardens and fountains up ahead. Listen out for the tap, tap, tap of the green woodpeckers that nest

Green
Woodpecker

in the gardens. Turn left before you get to the gate and walk all the way back up to the Diana Memorial Playground. Be ready for combat against a ship full of pirates and Captain Hook! Once he is safely in the jaws of the crocodile you can sail home.

9. Exit by Black Lion Gate, cross over, turn right and walk down to the corner of Bayswater and Leinster Terrace to see the plaque on J.M. Barrie's house. Then head back up Bayswater to Queensway and home for tea of fairy cakes coated with a healthy sprinkling of fairy dust.

Eat me, drink me
The park is perfect for picnics; otherwise, there are plenty of cafés.

Useful information
- Kensington Gardens 020 7298 2000 www.royalparks.org.uk
- Kensington Palace 0844 482 7777 www.hrp.org.uk
- The Serpentine Lido, with paddling pool, adults £4, children free. 020 7706 3422 www.serpentinelido.com

Books to read
By J.M. Barrie: *Peter Pan, Peter Pan in Kensington Gardens, The Little White Bird, Peter and Wendy*

Did you know?
- In 1929 Barrie took the cast of a London production of *Peter Pan* to the Great Ormond Street Hospital, where they performed the nursery scene.
- Wendy houses got their name from Wendy Darling; when she was injured in Neverland, Peter Pan and the Lost Boys built a small house around her where she had fallen.
- You can visit the house where J.M. Barrie was born in Angus, Scotland. 0844 493 2142 www.nts.org.uk

18. Shakespeare's city

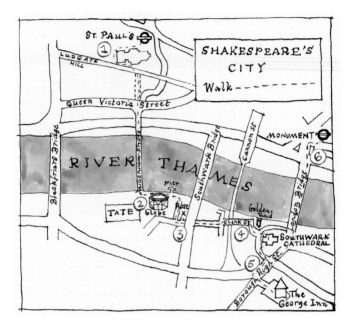

The Adventure

William Shakespeare was the great Elizabethan playwright, and perhaps the greatest playwright the English language has ever known. An actor as well as a writer, he lived among the brothels, prisons (including The Clink) and ale houses of Southwark. It was here that many of his plays were first performed, in some of England's earliest theatres.

In medieval times – indeed, well into the Elizabethan era and even beyond – plays were performed wherever a stage could be set up, which might be an inn yard, a rich man's palace, a hall such as that of the Middle Temple, even a cart on the street. The first recorded permanent theatres in London were built in the 1570s. Southwark on the south bank of the Thames, out of the reach of the puritanical City fathers, was a favoured location and the Swan, the Rose and the Globe were all built here in the late sixteenth century. A flag would be flown above the theatre when a play was to be performed, so those working in the City could make their way across the river to see it. Over a thousand people could squeeze in, standing in the centre as groundlings or 'stinkards', with more in the seating to the sides. At the end of a performance the bells of St Paul's Cathedral would chime to call everyone back to work.

Shakespearean Phrases We Use Today

Many of the words and phrases written by Shakespeare have now become part of the everyday English language.

A laughing stock (*The Merry Wives of Windsor*)
A sorry sight (*Macbeth*)
All that glitters is not gold (*The Merchant of Venice*)
All the world's a stage (*As You Like It*)
As dead as a doornail (*Henry VI, Part II*)
Brave new world (*The Tempest*)
Eaten out of house and home (*Henry IV, Part II*)
In a pickle (*The Tempest*)
In the twinkling of an eye (*The Merchant Of Venice*)
I will wear my heart upon my sleeve (*Othello*)
Mum's the word (*Henry VI, Part II*)
Neither here nor there (*Othello*)
Send him packing (*Henry IV, Part I*)
Set your teeth on edge (*Henry IV, Part I*)
There's method in my madness (*Hamlet*)
Too much of a good thing (*As You Like It*)
Vanish into thin air (*Othello*)

This walk takes you along the Thames past Shakespeare's haunts – the reconstructed Globe theatre, the remains of the Rose theatre, Borough Market and Southwark Cathedral, the Elizabethan George Inn – and across the river the way his audiences would have come, over London Bridge.

Shakespeare

How far? 3.2 km/2 miles
Start St Paul's tube **Finish** Monument tube

Walk the Walk

1. Leave the tube station by exit 2. Turn left down Panyer Alley and right on to St Paul's Churchyard. Walk all the way around to the other side of the Cathedral and cross at the lights to the pedestrianized St Peter's Hill. Cross Queen Victoria Street just beside the College of Arms. Walk straight on to the Millennium Footbridge and over the River Thames.

2. Head for the Globe theatre just ahead of you, to the left of Tate Modern. Thanks to the energies of the American film director and actor Sam Wanamaker, Shakespeare's Globe was faithfully reconstructed on almost exactly the original site – just slightly closer to the river's edge. The

Globe Theatre East Tower

original Globe theatre burned to the ground in 1613, after a spark from a cannon fired for dramatic effect caught in the thatched roof. At the Globe, admire the outside, take a peek in the courtyard, wander through the shop and exhibition areas, or buy a ticket for the full tour.

3. When you are done, turn right, walking east along the river footpath, and turn right shortly into Bear Gardens, looking out for the old Ferryman's seat in the wall. Turn left into Park Street, passing a plaque marking the original site of the Rose theatre on the left. Walk under Southwark Bridge to a rather forlorn plaque marking the exact spot of the original Globe, on the other side of the road. At the end of the street turn left, then immediately right down Clink Street, passing the old prison site, now a Museum of Horror and Torture. The cobbled streets take you past the ruins of Winchester Palace, with its fine rose window.

4. The path meanders through Pickford's Wharf, passing a replica of Sir Francis Drake's ship, the *Golden Hinde*. As the path then bends to the left, you will see Southwark Cathedral ahead of you. Walk through the modern doorway of the Cathedral and take an immediate right into the old church. This was Shakespeare's church and his brother is buried here. Look for the plaque behind the altar. There is also a 1911 memorial figure of William Shakespeare, with stained glass windows above telling the stories from his plays, that's worth hunting down. Leave by the exit opposite to the one you came in by, and turn right up the steps and left out on to Cathedral Street.

To either side of you is Borough Market, the oldest market in London, dating back to 1014. It is now a brilliant food market, selling organic meats, delicious cheeses, fresh fruit and vegetables (open Thursdays, Fridays and Saturdays). It is a great place to stop and explore.

5. Walk on to the main road ahead, Borough High Street, and turn right. Cross Southwark Street and then cross Borough High Street. Turn right. Shortly on your left is the George Inn, the last remaining galleried coaching inn in London, now looked

Shakespeare's Plays

Comedies
All's Well That Ends Well
As You Like It
The Comedy of Errors
Love's Labour's Lost
Measure for Measure
The Merchant of Venice
The Merry Wives of Windsor
A Midsummer Night's Dream
Much Ado about Nothing
The Taming of the Shrew
Twelfth Night
The Two Gentlemen of Verona
Histories
Henry IV, Part I
Henry IV, Part II
Henry V
Henry VI, Part I
Henry VI, Part II
Henry VI, Part III
Henry VIII

King John
Richard II
Richard III
Tragedies
Antony and Cleopatra
Coriolanus
Hamlet
Julius Caesar
King Lear
Macbeth
Othello
Romeo and Juliet
Timon of Athens
Titus Andronicus
Troilus and Cressida
Late Romances
Cymbeline
Pericles
The Tempest
The Winter's Tale

after by the National Trust. It is just the kind of pub that Shakespeare would have performed in before the theatres were built.

6. Retrace your steps up Borough High Street, this time heading towards the river. Cross the Thames into the City over London Bridge, as the people who came to see Shakespeare's plays would have done. Turn right at Monument Street and take the tube at Monument station.

Eat me, drink me

Borough Market has many good places to eat, and the riverfront has a selection of restaurants. Or take a picnic and find a spot by the river to eat and watch the boats go by.

Useful information

- The Globe 020 7902 1400 www.shakespeares-globe.org
- The Rose. Special arrangements can be made to see the remains of the Rose theatre, not normally open to the public. www.rosetheatre.org.uk
- Borough Market, open Thursday and Friday afternoons and on Saturdays www.boroughmarket.org.uk
- The George Inn 020 7407 2056 www.nationaltrust.org.uk

Did you know?

- William Shakespeare died a rich man and is buried in Holy Trinity church, Stratford upon Avon.
- The Elizabethans didn't wash their clothes – they just hung them on the line to air.
- Urine was collected and fermented for three weeks and used as a stain remover. Pregnant women's urine was sought after as the high oestrogen content made it particularly effective.

19. Henry VIII's court at Hampton

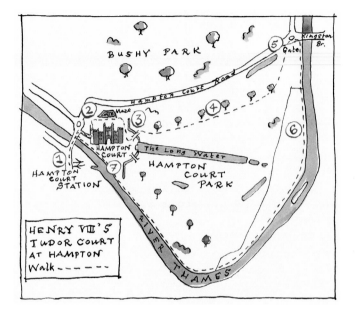

BUSHY PARK

Kingston Br.

Gate

Hampton Court Road

Maze

HAMPTON COURT

The Long Water

HAMPTON COURT PARK

HAMPTON COURT STATION

RIVER THAMES

HENRY VIII'S TUDOR COURT AT HAMPTON Walk - - - - -

The Adventure

Hampton Court Palace was the most sumptuous of all Henry VIII's palaces. The previous occupant, Cardinal Wolsey, had transformed a grand but relatively simple private house into a magnificent palace which aroused Henry's envy. After the King commandeered it in 1528 he spent more than ten years refurbishing and rebuilding it until it was the most modern palace in all England. It was sophisticated in taste and cultured in style, with pleasure gardens, a chapel, dining rooms, tennis courts, bowling alleys, a hunting park and a lavatory – called the Great House of Easement – that could seat twenty-eight. Hampton Court was home to each of Henry's wives in turn, and to his three children and the 1,200 members of his Court.

Hampton Court Palace is a series of courtyards and courts, kitchens, a chapel and outbuildings, all joined across this vast site. The West Gatehouse is Tudor, as are Henry VIII's State Apartments. Later, in 1689, William and Mary commissioned Christopher Wren to build a baroque palace on the side of the Tudor palace, and that's mostly what you can see from the outside. If you want to see just the Tudor places, head for the Tudor Gatehouse, the Henry VIII Great Hall, the Young Henry VIII exhibition, the Chapel Royal and the Tudor Kitchens. This will be more than enough for one visit in any case. This walk takes you through the palace, past the famous maze and out through Home Park, one of Henry's hunting grounds, along the River Thames, looping back to the palace and its glorious gilded gates.

How far? 8 km/5 miles
Start and finish Hampton Court station

Walk the Walk

1. From the station, turn right towards the river and cross Hampton Court Bridge. Hampton Court Palace is on your right. There are great views of its glory as you approach. Walk up the driveway through the palace gates. The ticket office is on your left, if you want to buy a full ticket to see the palace, or just a ticket for the Formal Gardens (free in winter) and the Maze. Otherwise, you can explore much of the outside for free, including the Gatehouse and Home Park. Start the walk at the Tudor Gatehouse. Note the English Lion and the Unicorn above it. Count the number of griffins, dragons, dogs and lions on the posts around the entrance. Facing the entrance, turn left on the path in front of it, between the main palace and the outbuildings. Follow the signs to the Tiltyard Café to get yourself in the right direction, passing through a rose garden.

HENRY VIII'S WIVES

Katherine of Aragon
(Divorced)

Anne Boleyn
(Beheaded)

Jane Seymour
(Died)

Anne of Cleves
(Divorced)

Katherine Howard
(Beheaded)

Katherine Parr
(Survived)

2. Before the café, take the gateway into an area of the park called the Wilderness. Follow the signs to the famous Hampton Court Maze, planted in 1690 by William III and used as a courtly entertainment. The paths cover a third of an acre and over half a mile of twists and turns. You can also buy a ticket here. It usually takes about twenty minutes to get to the centre, though it may well entertain you for much longer.

3. Leaving the maze, turn left through the Wilderness into the Formal Gardens. There is another ticket booth here at the entrance. In the Formal Gardens, follow the curved path round to the other side of the palace, then turn left to cross the first footbridge, and through the gate into Home Park.

If you have a dog, or if you don't have a ticket (needed in summer only) for the Formal Gardens, you will have to take a slight detour: leave the Wilderness by turning left through Lion Gate, then turn right along Hampton Court Road. Walk past Ivy Cottage and turn through Paddock's Gate on the right. Follow the wooden fencing, and enter Home Park, on the far side of the Palace. Head left, leaving the palace behind you.

Home Park is the 303 hectares/750 acres of wild grassy land ahead of you. The park has over three hundred deer, direct descendants of those introduced by Henry VIII for hunting. Wildlife flourishes in the park, with ant colonies, oak moths, bats, grey herons, and skylarks. Imagine you are tracking the deer and get the children to see how close they can get to the grazing herds.

fallow deer

The Tudor Dynasty

The Tudors were a Royal dynasty that began when Henry Tudor defeated King Richard III at the Battle of Bosworth in 1485. His son, Henry VIII, was only seventeen when he came to the throne. He was a tall, clever, musical and athletic man.

Henry has a bad reputation as a serial husband, but in fact he was married to Katherine of Aragon for nearly twenty-four years, longer than all his other wives put together. Henry and Katherine had six children, but only Mary survived. In desperate hope of having a male heir, he married again and again, producing only one son to survive childhood. Edward became King of England at the age of nine. He died six years later.

4. Walk alongside the wall, then straight ahead through the avenue of lime trees. Walk straight on, keeping a distant church tower in your sights. In ten minutes or so you will pass Wick Pond.

5. Keep going through the long grass on mown paths until you reach the tarmac (cars drive here) and leave the park by Kingston Gate on the left, passing an ice-house where they once kept the meat, fish and puddings fresh for the palace.

6. Turn right on the main road, walking towards the roundabout and Kingston Bridge. Just before the bridge is Barge Walk, a path down to the right. The signpost says three miles to Hampton Court. Turn here. The path is easy to follow and takes you all the way back to Hampton Court along the river. Keep everyone amused by looking at the boats, the sailing clubs and the swans.

Tudor Rose

7. Eventually the path turns a corner to reveal the golden gates of Hampton Court Palace. Cross back over the bridge to get back to the station.

cooking in Tudor Times

The fabulous kitchens at Hampton Court Palace were never busier than in the reign of the Tudors. The court had over 1,200 people to feed every day. Spices imported from the East and from Europe were used to flavour the royal dishes, along with English mustard, herbs from the Palace gardens and fruit from the orchards. There were three vast larders to store the food and the kitchens had six fireplaces. In a typical year, the Elizabethan court ate 1,240 oxen, 8,200 sheep, 2,330 deer, 760 calves, 1,870 pigs and 53 wild boar, and washed it all down with 600,000 gallons of beer.

Eat me, drink me
The Tiltyard Café at Hampton Court is good. Or take a picnic to eat in Home Park or by the river.

Useful information
- Hampton Court Palace. Information and advance tickets 0844 482 7799 www.hrp.org.uk
- Arrive or leave as the Tudor royals did, by boat: Thames River Boats 020 7930 2062 www.wpsa.co.uk Turk Launches 020 8546 2434 www.turks.co.uk No services during the winter months.

Further afield
- Go to the National Portrait Gallery in Trafalgar Square if you want to see a splendid (and free) collection of Tudor portraits. 020 7312 2463 www.npg.org.uk
- Visit Henry VIII's warship, the *Mary Rose*, in Portsmouth. 023 9281 2931 www.maryrose.org

Books to read
- *A Traveller in Time* by Alison Uttley. The childhood classic of a little girl who travels back in time to a Tudor house.
- *The Prince and the Pauper* by Mark Twain. A chance encounter on the streets of Tudor London changes the lives of two boys.

Did you know?
- Hampton Court is thought to be haunted by the ghost of Henry's fifth wife, Katherine Howard. Put under house arrest because Henry suspected her of adultery, she escaped from her guards and ran screaming through the Long Gallery. She was caught and taken to the Tower for execution.

20. The Boat Race: Rowing on the Thames

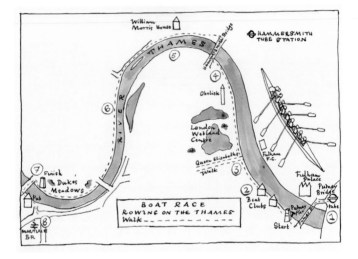

The Adventure

The famous Oxford and Cambridge Boat Race starts near Putney Bridge and ends just downstream of Barnes Bridge. The first race was held in 1829 at Henley-on-Thames and some later races took place at Westminster. It was in 1845 that the Boat Race moved to the country village of Putney. The course is 4 miles and 374 yards and is rowed in boats called eights, because they are designed for eight rowers (plus a cox to steer). The fastest time recorded is 16 minutes and 19 seconds by the Cambridge crew in 1998, breaking the previous record by 26 seconds. Follow the entire course from the towpath, ticking off the landmarks that keep the rowers going. Experience the river close up as it loops up to Hammersmith and back down to Barnes. This stretch of the river is busy in all seasons, all weathers and all tides. Dotted along its banks are the boathouses of famous rowing clubs, their yards stacked with sleek slim-line boats or 'shells'. Explore the shoreline and watch the birds in the river sanctuaries, set alongside some of London's prettiest houses dating from a time when Hammersmith and Chiswick were still small country villages. Don't forget to cheer when you reach the finishing post.

How far? 7 km/4½ miles
Start Putney Bridge tube **Finish** Mortlake station

Walk the Walk

1. Turn left out of the tube station and take the alley by the railway signposted to the Thames Path. Don't go under the arch. Keep right to the river's edge and at Putney Bridge dog-leg right and then left to find the stairs. Cross the bridge to the other side of the river. Turn right and walk down the Lower Richmond Road. Veer right to the riverside path. Look across to the other bank to see Bishop's Park, the gardens of Fulham Palace, which was the country house of the Bishops of London for over thirteen hundred years. But don't be too busy looking to notice, just before Putney Pier, the University Stone, which marks the start line of the Oxford and Cambridge Boat Race.

2. Shortly afterwards, when the pavement gives way to a tarmac lane, comes a chandlery and a clutch of famous boat club houses including the ones used by the crews in the Boat Race. The Oxford crew uses the Westminster School Boat Club House and the Cambridge crew uses the King's College School Boat Club House. The boats row to the marker you've just seen and line up their bows before the start of the race. Walk past Leander Gardens and along the towpath, taking you past the Barn Elms Boathouse.

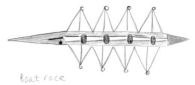

Boat race

Rowing Speak

Blades oars
Catch put the blade in the water
Easy oars stop rowing
Ergo indoor rowing machine
Finish take blade out of the water
Gate the bit the blade sits in
Push make more effort
Riggers the metal bit bolted on the side of the boat
Rowing one oar per person
Sculling two oars per person
Shells boats

3. Keep going and you eventually pass Queen Elizabeth Walk (turn up here if you are interested in visiting the Barnes Wetland Centre about ten minutes away). Opposite is Craven Cottage, home of Fulham Football Club since 1896, and one of the markers on the Boat Race course. Look out along the river for people practising their rowing. Just before you get to the Harrods Village find the obelisk memorial to Steve Fairbairn, a nineteenth-century rower who founded the Head of the River Race, another famous rowing race for eights rowed over the same course as the Boat Race, but in reverse; from Mortlake to Putney. This is also the one mile marker to the start of the Oxford and Cambridge Boat Race. You should see a stone here bearing the initials UBR (University Boat Race).

4. Walk on to Hammersmith Bridge, a suspension bridge spanning 128.5m/422ft. In 1992 a weight limit was placed on it, and heavy vehicles and double-decker buses are now banned from using it. Cross to the other side of the river and take the ramp

Black-headed Gull

down to the path. Continue going west along the Thames Path towards Barnes Bridge and Mortlake through Furnival Gardens and on to Upper Mall, where you will walk by some of the prettiest and oldest houses in London. You will pass the quaint Dove pub (no children allowed) on your left and just beyond here, on your right is Kelmscott House, the beautiful Georgian house where social reformer, designer and founder of the Arts and Crafts Movement William Morris lived. Morris found the Thames hugely inspiring, and many of his designs are named after its tributaries: the Wandle, the Medway and the Lea for example. He was also keen on boating and used to travel to his house in Oxfordshire along the river. It took him a week and he kept a diary and wrote a poem about it. The house is now home to the William Morris Society and it opens twice a week, on Thursday and Saturday afternoons.

As you walk, look across the river towards Barnes and you should see St Paul's Boys' School boathouse and on this side the London Corinthian Sailing Club, founded in 1894. Keep going along the river's edge, past the Old Ship pub, until you are forced right at the Black Lion pub.

5. Turn left into Hammersmith Terrace, which until the 1860s was still bordered by market gardens; by the early twentieth century these had been replaced by waterworks, breweries and timber wharves. Because of the stunning location it attracted many artists and artisans: notice the many blue plaques remembering them all. No. 7, Emery Walker's former home, is open to the public.

6. Walk along the exquisite Chiswick Mall and look out for the Church Street Causeway at the end on the left. When the tide

is out take this opportunity to go down to the river and a tiny slip of an island called the Chiswick Eyot. Grass and osiers (willow) were once cultivated here and used for basketry, furniture, cart-making and cattle fodder. The green pole at one end is another of the rowers' landmarks along the route. As you come back up the causeway, take the first left following a Thames Path sign past some houses and back to the river, where you might see some RNLI boats moored at Chiswick Pier. Keep going along the paved path and eventually you will come to Duke's Meadows. This is an altogether leafier bit of the river lined with elder bushes (good for making cordial). Things you will pass on the way include a heron's nest sculpture and some faded Edwardian bandstands.

7. As you approach Barnes Bridge, you will be diverted away from the river with a right turn. Follow the Thames Path sign along the road. At the Riverside Health Club turn left under a railway arch. Continue along the road, past Duke's Hollow Nature Reserve and Chiswick Boathouse. Take the left, marked Thames Path, through the yard and follow the path back to the river's edge. In spring, this path is edged with cow parsley and bright yellow mustard flowers. Keep going until you arrive at the dark and light blue striped finishing post ahead of Chiswick Bridge. Cut through the Tideway Scullers School Boatyard and out to the steps of Chiswick Bridge. Cross the river.

8. Take the first steps down to the left, turn right and follow signs to Mortlake station, a short walk away. You will pass some more pretty riverside houses and the Ship pub. Turn right here, walking between the pub and the brewery, still following signs to Mortlake station. At the top of Ship Lane cross over Lower Richmond Road, cut diagonally across the park and turn right to the station.

Heron

Eat me, drink me

Enjoy a pub lunch on the way, at either the Black
Lion (020 8748 2639) or the Ship at Mortlake
(020 8876 1439) or have a riverside picnic.

Useful information

- Oxford and Cambridge Boat Race
  www.theboatrace.org
- British Rowing offers rowing lessons to children aged eleven
  upwards. 020 8237 6700 www.british-rowing.org
- The Marine Society and Sea Cadets is a nationwide voluntary
  youth organization for ten to eighteen year olds.
  020 7654 7000 www.ms-sc.org
- The Barnes Wetland Centre 020 8409 4400 www.wwt.org.uk
- The William Morris Society
  020 8741 3735 www.morrissociety.org.
- Emery Walker House 020 8741 4104 www.emerywalker.org.uk

Books to read

- *Three Men in a Boat* by Jerome K. Jerome. A funny nineteenth-
  century story of a holiday on the Thames in a skiff.
- 'Growltiger's last Stand', the story of a cat who lived on a barge
  which travelled up and down the Thames, from *Old Possum's
  Book of Practical Cats* by T.S. Eliot.

Did you know?

- As of 2009 Cambridge leads with 79 wins, against Oxford's 74.
  Cambridge has been the front-runner since 1829.
- It is traditional for the loser of the Boat Race to challenge the
  winner to the following year's Race.
- Up until 2009 the Cambridge boat has sunk three times and the
  Oxford boat twice.

21. Florence Nightingale and the Story of Medicine

The Adventure

Florence Nightingale was born in 1820 and named after the city of her birth. The daughter of wealthy parents, she became a nurse, although at the time it was frowned upon for young ladies to work. During the Crimean War of 1853–6 she was commissioned by the Ministry of War to go to the Crimea, where the hospitals were basic, filthy and overcrowded. This meant that the wounded soldiers were catching diseases like typhus, cholera and dysentery and more were dying from these diseases than from their wounds. Florence Nightingale believed, as did many at the time, that it was a 'miasma' or 'bad air' which caused infection. Although this wasn't the case, cleaning the field hospitals got rid of the bad bacteria secreted in the dirt and made it much less likely that the soldiers would get infections. At night Nightingale would tour the wards to comfort the soldiers carrying a lantern, which is how she got her nickname of 'the lady with the lamp'. On her return to London, Florence Nightingale was quite a celebrity. She campaigned for better quality of nursing in hospitals, advised on sanitation and in 1859 published her *Notes on Nursing*, which is still in print. A school of nursing was opened in her name at St Thomas's hospital. It is largely because of Florence Nightingale that we wash our hands before we eat or after we go to the toilet, to stop the spread of infection. Visit a museum dedicated to Nightingale and the history of nursing, investigate the Crimean War at the National Army Museum and explore herbal medicine at a 300-year-old garden (check opening times before you go). Walk this way to follow in the footsteps of an extraordinary Victorian woman.

How far? 6.4 km/4 miles
Start Westminster tube **Finish** Sloane Square tube

Walk the Walk
1. Take exit 1 signposted Westminster Pier. Take the steps up to Westminster Bridge and cross Bridge Street and the bridge.

What You'd Expect to Find in a Victorian Medicine Chest

Aromatic confection made from cinnamon, cardamom, ginger and orange peel: digestion aid
Aspirin (from willow): for pain relief
Jamaican ginger: a tonic
Quinine: for fevers
Rhubarb pills: a laxative
Tincture of digitalis (from foxglove): for dropsy
Tincture of opium: a painkiller
Turkey rhubarb: a laxative
Wine of ipecacuanha: a purgative and emetic

Turn right into a walkway to St Thomas's Hospital. Just before the main entrance take a small set of stairs on your right down to the car park. Carry on straight ahead to the newly refurbished Florence Nightingale Museum on the left. Here you can learn all about Florence Nightingale, the Crimean War, health care in Victorian times, and the story of nursing. Look out for the slate Florence used as a child, her pet owl Athena, and a Turkish lantern like the ones used in the Crimean War. You will also learn about Mary Seacole, another nurse who made a great contribution to the welfare of the soldiers in the Crimea. Exit the museum and retrace your steps towards Westminster Bridge. Don't cross back over the river but turn left, taking the steps to the riverside path. Follow the Thames Path all the way to Lambeth Bridge.

2. Cross over Lambeth Palace Road at Lambeth Palace, home of the Archbishop of Canterbury. Pop next door to the Garden Museum to look at a herbarium – a volume of dried plant specimens. Florence Nightingale had one. Botanists today at places like Kew Gardens and the Natural History Museum still use herbaria as references, and substances derived from plants are the basis of many modern drugs.

    Exiting the museum, turn left and then left again down Lambeth Road to the zebra crossing. Go straight over into the Royal Pharmaceutical Society building. In the nineteenth century, this Society ran an annual competition for the best herbarium. Although the majority of the specimens of flora and fauna collected by the Society are now at Kew Gardens, the museum in the foyer here (open Monday to Friday) has an entire case dedicated to pharmacy and nature.

Florence nightingale

3. Exit and return to Lambeth Bridge and London's best view of the Houses of Parliament. Cross over the bridge and over Millbank, continuing

up Horseferry Road. Turn left down Dean Ryle Street and into John Islip Street. Continue for approximately half a mile to Vauxhall Bridge Road. Cross the road, take the first turning left into Drummond Gate, then round the bend to Bessborough Street, passing Pimlico tube. This next stretch is a further half mile. If this sounds too much, take the tube to Sloane Square and walk down Lower Sloane Street to the Royal Hospital Chelsea. Otherwise, continue along Lupus Street (full of good shops for snacks) to Grosvenor Road and the river.

4. At Grosvenor Road turn right past the pumping station built in response to the 'great stink' of 1858, when the smell of untreated sewage so overwhelmed central London that government ground to a halt. Cross over Chelsea Bridge Road and keep walking to the Bull Ring Gate entrance of Ranelagh Gardens. This leads to the Royal Hospital, home since 1682 to the Chelsea Pensioners, instantly recognizable by the distinctive scarlet coats and tricorne hats they wear on ceremonial occasions. Up ahead you will see a golden statue of Charles II, who commissioned Wren to build this institution for the 'succour and relief of veterans broken by age and war'. The building is open to the public and a good spot to enjoy a picnic and rest weary feet.

Medicinal Herbs

Angelica: for respiratory diseases
Centaury: to heal wounds
Comfrey: a painkiller
Common rue: a general cure-all
Coriander: used with dill and sage for jaundice
Fennel: for eye diseases
Lovage: for asthma, dropsy, gout, snakebites, sore throat and stomach troubles

5. Follow the path, turning left and then round to the right. Exit from the gates up ahead on to Royal Hospital Road. Turn left past the National Army Museum (save your visit until later) and left down Swan Walk and through the flower-covered entrance to the Chelsea Physic Garden, founded in 1673 as the Apothecaries' Garden, with the purpose of training apprentices in identifying plants. Find the pharmaceutical garden filled with plants used to help cure ailments. Don't touch – they may be poisonous.

Retrace your steps to the National Army Museum and nip in to try on some soldiers' uniforms, see Florence Nightingale's medals and learn lots more about the Crimean War, which is famous for such disastrous episodes as the Charge of the Light Brigade, commemorated in Tennyson's poem.

6. Walk back past the impressive façade of the Royal Hospital to the junction with Chelsea Bridge Road. Cross over here and walk up Pimlico Road, then left along Holbein Place up to Sloane Square tube.

Eat me, drink me

The Museum of Garden History and the Chelsea Physic Garden both have lovely cafés. The Royal Hospital gardens provide an ideal picnic spot, except during the Chelsea Flower Show in May, when they're closed.

Useful information

- Florence Nightingale Museum 020 7620 0374
  www.florence-nightingale.co.uk
- The Garden Museum 020 7401 8865
  www.museumgardenhistory.org
- The Chelsea Physic Garden 020 7352 5646
  www.chelseaphysicgarden.co.uk

How to Make a Herbarium

You will need scissors, a specimen bag, a sketch book or some A4 sheets of cartridge paper, and PVA glue. Gather flowers, trying to avoid ones that are wet, and put them into your bag. Carefully stick down your specimens, one on each page, laying them out so you can see as much as possible of the plant. Large seeds and reproductive parts can be attached in a small envelope. Write a label and put this in the bottom right-hand corner of the page. Add maps or photographs showing where you found the specimen. To give the herbarium scientific value every plant needs information about where and when it was found and what the surrounding habitat was like.

- National Army Museum
  020 7734 3922 www.national-army-museum.ac.uk
- The Royal Hospital Chelsea 020 7881 5200
  www.chelsea-pensioners.co.uk.
- The Royal Pharmaceutical Society Museum, free admission.
  020 7572 2210 www.rpsgb.org.uk
- For all other medical museums in London including the Old
  Operating Theatre and Herb Garret at London Bridge, see
  www.medicalmuseums.org.

Books to read
- *Florence Nightingale: The Lady with the Lamp*
  by Charlotte Moore
- *Wonderful Adventures of Mrs. Seacole in Many Lands*
  by Mary Seacole
- 'The Charge of the Light Brigade', in *The Works of Alfred,
  Lord Tennyson*
- *Flashman at the Charge* by George MacDonald Fraser

Did you know?
- Alexis Soyer, a chef, went to the Crimea to improve the
  soldier's diet. He designed a special battlefield portable stove
  and wrote a cook book called *A Culinary Campaign*.
- As well as being a great administrator, Florence Nightingale
  was a brilliant statistician: she invented pie charts as a way
  of presenting figures in a meaningful and easy-to-read way.
- Florence Nightingale was a great campaigner and although
  there were no women in the House of Commons she made
  her views heard through her
  influential friends, so much
  so that Sir Harry Verney was
  nicknamed 'the member for
  Florence Nightingale'.

22. Meadows on the Thames at Royal Richmond

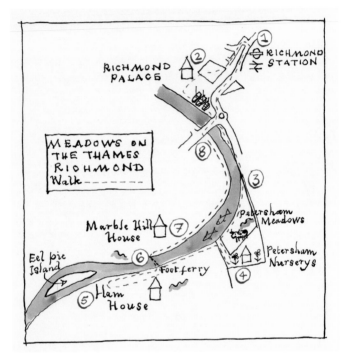

The Adventure

Royal Richmond was a favoured country retreat for busy Tudor and Stuart kings and queens and their courtiers. It benefited from easy access from the busy city via the river and provided good hunting. Similarly, artists and writers flocked to this riverside idyll. Designated as an 'arcadia' in the eighteenth century, even the view from Richmond Hill has been protected by an Act of Parliament. The river is still a key transport route, if only for the marine habitats along the Thames Estuary. Although Richmond is now part of London's sprawling metropolis it still has a convincing village feel to it. This is a place to relax, listen to birdsong, sketch, or fish. Come prepared for a lazy day in the country at Petersham Meadow and experience the historic equivalent of royal weekend hideaways, taking in a Tudor palace, a Stuart mansion and a Georgian villa. Cross the river by the oldest method possible: via foot ferry (in summer only), the only one still in operation on the tidal Thames. Bring a sketch book, fishing gear and a picnic.

How far? 6.4 km/4 miles
Start and finish Richmond tube and station

Walk the Walk

1. Exit Richmond station, turn right and cross The Quadrant at the lights. Turn right and almost immediately left down a passageway into Little Green. Turn left towards Richmond Theatre. Cut diagonally across Little Green and Richmond Green to the far corner. In Tudor times this was a popular venue for jousting. Cricket has been played here since the 1600s.

2. All that remains of Richmond Palace lies straight ahead. Henry VII built Richmond Palace on the site of the former Palace of Shene, which had burnt down. Henry VIII lived here until he moved to Hampton Court Palace, and Elizabeth I died here. The gateway is the only surviving part of the original building; it would have had enormous doors covering it. The pretty Georgian terrace of houses to the left of the Palace is Maids of Honour Row, which was built for the maids of Queen Caroline, wife of George II. Walk through the gateway down Old Palace Yard.

Elizabeth I[?]

3. Pass Trumpeters, a house built about 1700, and walk towards the corner,

following the fingerpost to the river. Turn left on Old Palace Lane, passing the White Swan pub and the Old Deer Park, once the Palace hunting ground. At the river turn left along Cholmondeley Walk. Dating from the eighteenth century, it is one of the oldest river paths in the country and was originally split into an upper and lower path: the lower, wetter path designated for tradesmen.

Shortly you will come to some artisans' workshops and boat makers. Traditional round-bottomed, clinker-built rowing boats or skiffs are still made here and can easily be hired for small outings (like when Ratty took Mole on his first trip upriver in *Wind in the Willows*). For the more adventurous, there are covered boats for camping out available from Richmond Bridge Boathouses. Richmond Bridge, built between 1774 and 1777, is the oldest surviving bridge over the Thames in London. The artist William Turner regularly painted the river here: visit the Turner Gallery at Tate Britain to see his work.

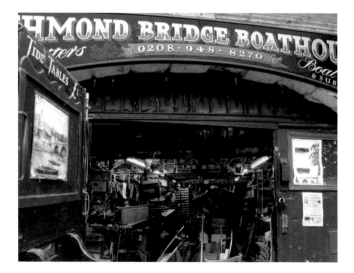

Butter cup

Continue on past Friars Lane and Water Lane all the way along the riverside path until you reach Buccleugh Gardens (there is a public toilet here). Cut through the gardens and at the far side follow the footpath back to the river's edge, direction Ham House. Petersham Meadows abuts the path here. A traditional flood meadow habitat, unusual in London because most of the river is purposely restricted from flooding, it is full of wild flowers: snake's head fritillary; orchids; adder's tongue; fern; meadow sweet; ragged robin and lots of buttercups. Traditional hedgerows of hawthorn, dog rose, field maple, damson and sloe are being planted around the perimeter with their branches layered to provide a barrier preventing the cattle from escaping and offering a secure place for birds to nest. Look out for flocks of lapwing and redshank which feed on the meadow. If you want to fish, this is the place to do so. A permit is not required over and above the usual licence. The best time to drop your line is five hours after high tide at London Bridge during the summer months, and four hours in the winter. You might catch roach, bream, perch, barbel or carp.

4. At the end of the meadow, follow the sign to Petersham for a short detour along River Lane to the lovely Petersham Nurseries for a gardening treat or something delicious to eat. Pass the Old Stables on your left and turn left down a small passageway signposted Petersham Nurseries. Follow it to the end. To continue the walk, retrace your steps to the river and turn left.

5. Walk on to Ham House, a short distance ahead. Bats are a common feature here at dusk as the scrub and woodland are an ideal habitat and it is well positioned for them to feast on the midges and mosquitoes that hang about the water. A bat can eat as many as two thousand insects in one night. Stop at Ham House, an ideal picnic spot, and have a look around. Built in 1610, it is an unusually intact Stuart mansion with

lavish seventeenth-century interiors. The gardens are great for hide and seek.

Carry on along the towpath until you can see Eel Pie Island, which provides a safe roosting habitat for waterfowl and some sea birds, including common terns and sand martins. It is also known for being the hangout of rock stars. Scenes for *The African Queen*, staring Humphrey Bogart and Katharine Hepburn, were also shot here and legend has it that two ring-necked parakeets escaped during filming. Now there are thousands of them along the river.

6. Turn around and walk back past Ham House. Don't go too far as you are looking for a small signpost and landing platform to catch Hammerton's Foot Ferry to the other side (operational between March and the end of October). If the ferry is not running, retrace your steps to Richmond.

7. Once over the other side, turn right and take the Thames Path to Richmond Bridge, passing a spectacular Palladian villa, Marble Hill House, on the way. It was built in the 1720s for Henrietta Howard, Countess of Suffolk and mistress to George II, who

RIVER FISH

Barbel

Bream

Brown Trout

Carp

Gudgeon

Perch

Pike

Roach

loved entertaining artists and poets. Alexander Pope and Jonathan Swift were among her guests.

8. Keep walking to the Richmond Bridge and then cross over the river. Turn left into Hill Street, right into George Street and then straight up the Quadrant to Richmond station.

Eat me, drink me

Petersham Nurseries is a special place to eat. 020 8605 3627 www.petershamnurseries.com. Otherwise Ham House (summer only) has a café. On a nice day nothing much beats a riverbank picnic.

Useful information

- Hammerton's Foot Ferry, between March and October only and operating hours are tide dependent. 020 8892 9620
- Ham House 020 8940 0735 www.nationaltrust.org.uk
- Marble Hill House 020 8892 5115 www.english-heritage.org.uk
- Boat Hire Richmond Bridge Boathouses 020 8948 8270 www.richmondbridgeboathouses.com

Books to read

- *The Water Babies* by Charles Kingsley. A chimney sweep falls into the river after being chased by a well-to-do girl.
- *The Wind in the Willows* by Kenneth Grahame

Did you know?

- In 1625 Charles I brought his court here to escape the plague in London.
- Artist Vincent Van Gogh was curate at Petersham Church.
- The Thames is tidal all the way up to Teddington Lock.

23. Mary Poppins in Battersea Park

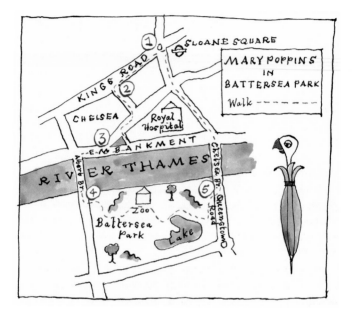

The Adventure

The London children's story about the magical and mysterious nanny Mary Poppins has captivated readers since it was first written in 1934. Eight Mary Poppins books were written in total, with the first famously telling the story of the arrival of the greatest children's nanny in literature. Made indelibly famous by the film with Julie Andrews as Mary herself, it tells the story of two children from the Banks family needing her care in their home at No. 17 Cherry Tree Lane.

As every mother knows, sadly there is no such creature as Mary Poppins, and there is

Pavement drawings

Take along some coloured chalk and, like Bert, fill the squares of London's pavements with drawings. Draw a chalk painting of a world you'd like to escape to, perhaps with green grass or a bit of blue sea, and a fairground in the background. Hold hands and jump in.

Practise saying
Supercalifragilisticexpialidocious

no street in London called Cherry Tree Lane. But it is possible to piece together elements of the stories and find the places of P.L. Travers inspiration and imagination. She lived at 50 Smith Street, Chelsea. The park described is almost certainly Battersea Park, just across the Thames, with its zoo and lakes. The East Wind blows in Mary Poppins by umbrella complete with her tardis-like carpet bag and impatient manner. Every child would dream of a nanny who rewards good behaviour with magic, can talk to animals and gives out medicine that tastes of everyone's favourite flavour (rum punch for Mary P.). The stories are full of Bert the Match Man (in the book) or chimney sweeps (in the film), laughing gas tea parties, pasting gingerbread stars to the sky, flying kites in the park and visiting old ladies who sell gingerbread whose fingers are made of barley-sugar. Take a kite and a rug for a picnic.

How far? 4 km/2½ miles
Start and finish Sloane Square tube

Walk the Walk

1. Spit spot, take a no-nonsense approach and stride out of Sloane Square tube, straight across the square towards Peter Jones and up the King's Road.

2. Some way down on your left, after Wellington Square, is Smith Street, where the Mary Poppins author, P.L. Travers, lived at No. 50. She apparently sent the Disney producers a photograph of her house when they were trying to re-create Cherry Tree Lane for the 1964 film.

3. Turn left and walk all the way down Smith Street, cross St Leonard's Terrace and continue down Ormonde Gate to Royal Hospital Road. Turn right here, heading for the Embankment. Turn left on the corner of Swan Walk and walk past the Chelsea Physic Garden, one of London's oldest gardens, tucked away behind a high wall.

4. Turn right along Chelsea Embankment, towards Albert Bridge. Cross the road and walk over the bridge. Take the first small gate into Battersea Park on your left. Make your way through the park, heading east. While there is no

Cherry Tree Lane in London with a park across the road, it is quite likely that P.L. Travers based her park on Battersea Park, with its small zoo, lake, wild corner and winding paths. Read *Mary Poppins in the Park* for a particularly eccentric tale of the adventures of the Banks children and their nanny, set in a park just like this one. Lay out your rug and picnic, sit bolt upright against a tree while the children play around you.

5. Walk through the park, exploring as you like, eventually coming out the opposite side on Queenstown Road. Like Mary Poppins and her charges, hop on a London bus. Take the 137 or 452 bus up Queenstown Road, over Chelsea Bridge and back to Sloane Square tube. You can, equally, if you're not too whacked, walk up the busy Chelsea Bridge Road and Lower Sloane Street to Sloane Square.

LONDON BIRDS

Blackbird

Blue Tit

Jay

Magpie

Parakeet

Pigeon

Robin

Thrush

Woodpecker

Raspberry Jam cakes

Fairy cakes sliced through and filled with raspberry jam would be just the ticket for a raspberry jam cake. Mary Poppins always ate these on her days out with Bert and they were her favourite kind of cake.

Eat me, drink me

Take a picnic to have in the park. Otherwise, Sloane Square is busy with places to eat. There is a good café, La Gondola al Parco, in Battersea Park by the lake.

Useful information

- Friends of Battersea Park www.batterseapark.org
- Battersea Park Children's Zoo 020 7924 5826
  www.batterseaparkzoo.co.uk.

Further afield

There are two other places worth seeing if you are keen on Mary Poppins. Neither could squeeze into this walk but they are easy to get to in London.

- Admiral Boom's House, Admiral's Walk, Hampstead NW3 (Hampstead tube). 'Blast my gizzard,' there is such a thing as the Admiral's House, built to look like a ship with a flag pole, quarter deck and curved windows. The house that P.L. Travers was inspired by is on the bend of this little road.

London Bus

- Feed the birds at St Paul's Cathedral (St Paul's tube). Walk up Ludgate Hill in the City and stop at the steps of St Paul's Cathedral, built a long time ago 'by a man with a bird's name' (Wren), as P.L. Travers writes, arguing this is why so many birds like to come here. You can't buy bird seed for tuppence a bag any longer, but you can sing 'Feed the Birds' when you get there – print out the lyrics from www.stlyrics.com before you go.

Books to read
The Mary Poppins books by P.L. Travers:
Mary Poppins, Mary Poppins Comes Back, Mary Poppins Opens the Door, Mary Poppins in the Park, Mary Poppins in the Kitchen, Mary Poppins A–Z, Mary Poppins in Cherry Tree Lane, Mary Poppins and the House Next Door

Did you know?
- The illustrations in the original Mary Poppins books were drawn by the artist Mary Shepard, daughter of the Winnie-the-Pooh illustrator E.H. Shepard.
- Walt Disney were originally thinking of casting Bette Davies as the cold but magical nanny.
- P.L. Travers so hated the film version of her book, she reputedly left the premiere in tears. She loathed the Americanism of 'go fly a kite' in the song.

24. The Story of Ice-cream and the Regent's canal

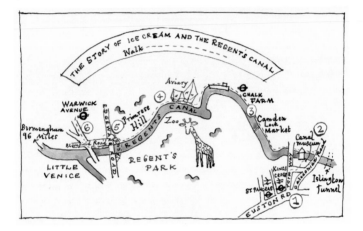

The Adventure

This walk is both an exploration of one of the finest stretches of the Regent's Canal, and the story of ice-cream in London. It was London's Italian community, who lived largely in Islington, Clerkenwell and King's Cross and traditionally worked the streets as organ-grinders, who took to making ice-cream. By the end of the nineteenth century, selling penny ices was the most popular job for Italian immigrants. London's canals were the magic ingredient that allowed all this to happen. In the days before electric freezers, ice had to be shipped from cold countries like Norway to London, and it was kept in ice wells deep in the ground by the side of the canals. The most famous of all London's ice-cream merchants, Carlo Gatti, cut his ice from vast ice wells in the Regent's Canal. In 1849 Gatti opened a café serving ice-creams and chocolate, and by 1860 he was recorded as an ice merchant at 2 New Wharf Road, where the Canal Museum is today.

Life on the canal

Whole families used to live and work on the canals. Parents would steer the barges and the children would walk the horses on the towpaths and work the locks, walking ahead to make them ready. Children mostly didn't go to school and couldn't read or write. They fished for eel and poached rabbit and pheasants. They decorated the barges with bright colours, roses and castles and good luck symbols. They painted jugs, tins and pots as well as the boats themselves.

The network of canals that runs through the centre of London and heads off across the English countryside was vital to the city's success and expansion in the eighteenth and nineteenth centuries. Great ships from all over the world would dock in the Docklands and unload their cargo on to canal boats. Pretty much made redundant by the advent of railways and motorways, the canals of London have, until recently been forgotten. But now they are having something of a renaissance as urban green spots, providing habitats for wildlife and a walking and cycling corridor for Londoners.

How far? 3.2 km/2 miles to Chalk Farm, 7 km/4½ miles to Warwick Avenue
Start King's Cross tube
Finish Chalk Farm tube or Warwick Avenue tube

Walk the Walk

1. Leave the tube by the Euston Road north side exit. Turn left, passing in front of the railway station, and then left again on to York Way. Walk up York Way and turn right on to Wharfdale Road.

Fox

How a canal Lock works

Canal boats can be raised or lowered from one level to another by means of a lock. The boat enters a special chamber with gates at each end. Once inside the chamber, the water from the other side of the gate is released to fill the chamber and raise the level of the boat to the same height as the continuing canal.

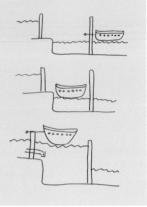

2. Take the second left down New Wharf Road, passing the rather wonderful Canal Museum tucked away on the left. This is a great museum and it is definitely worth stepping in for a quick visit. In its small space it has enough of interest to keep everyone entertained. You can peer into Gatti's original ice well and climb aboard a canal boat. To continue the walk, turn left out of the museum, right on All Saints Street, then left on to the Caledonian Road.

Walk over the canal bridge and then take a left through a gate to drop down to the towpath. If you look left, you can just see the start of the Islington Tunnel, the longest on the canal, which opened in 1820. The tunnel was a feat of engineering for its time and is perfectly straight. It is possible to see right through to the other end. It is three-quarters of a mile long and was too narrow to take horses through. Children would lead the horses overhead through Islington, while the men and women who worked on the barges would move the barge through the tunnel by 'legging' – lying on their backs and pushing against

the tunnel walls with their legs to drive it through. The Canal Museum organizes special tunnel trips once a month during the summer (you'll need to book in advance).

Turn right along the towpath towards Camden Town. The canal path needs little direction as it follows the water's edge. Interesting sights pepper the way. The gritty urban surroundings are to be transformed by the new King's Cross development, with art galleries, concert halls, shops and cafés. The waterway is a haven for London's wildlife and Camley Street Natural Park, one of London's wild reserves, backs on to the canal here, across the water. The canals are valuable green pathways through the city. Look out for dragonflies and damselflies, herons, kingfishers, cormorants, foxes, bats, toads and frogs.

The path comes to St Pancras Lock, where coal was unloaded to serve the railways. After several bridges, the path climbs up to the Hampstead Road Lock at Camden Market.

3. Dip in and out of Camden Market. The path takes you to the market square, a treasure trove for secondhand clothes and music. Under the railway arches are scores of takeaway Asian food stalls, juicing stalls, crêpe stalls and other opportunities to indulge. Depending on the size of the feet accompanying you on this walk, you can either peel off here, walking through the market, and turning left up Camden High Street and then Chalk Farm Road to Chalk Farm tube station; or pick up a canal boat at Camden Lock and take a fifty-minute boat ride to Little Venice. No need to book in advance. The boats run more or less every hour in the summer and regularly through winter.

4. For those walking on to Little Venice, go back to where you left off and pick up the canal path again in the far corner of the cobbled square at the Lock. Walk up and down the very steep bridge and on to Regent's Park and London Zoo. From the canal path, you can get a glimpse of the animals and a great view of the aviary designed by Lord Snowdon.

Make Lemon Ice

Ingredients
750ml water • 500g caster sugar
juice from 7 lemons • zest of 1 lemon

- Put the water and sugar in a pan and heat gently until the sugar has dissolved. Bring to the boil and then leave to cool down for a few minutes. Stir in the lemon juice and most of the zest.
- Churn the liquid in an ice-cream machine to turn it to sorbet.
- If you don't have an ice-cream maker, pour it into a container and put it in the freezer for about 5 hours. Stir regularly during the freezing process to break the crystals.
- Sprinkle with zest and serve.

5. The towpath wends its way for another mile or so, leaving the canal side briefly at the Maida Hill tunnel. Head up the steps and walk straight on down Aberdeen Place. Cross over the Edgware Road and straight on into Blomfield Road, walking alongside the canal barges.

6. Turn right at the lights towards Warwick Avenue tube station, which is shortly on your right. Or, now you are at Little Venice, drop down through the gate on the left, just before the bridge, to see where the Regent's and Grand Union Canals join. Then retrace your steps to the tube.

Eat me, drink me
Stop off at the many food stalls and cafés in Camden Market.

Kingfisher

Useful information
- The Canal Museum, King's Cross (closed Mondays) 020 7713 0836 www.canalmuseum.org.uk
- Hire a canal boat for the day with a skipper from Camden Narrowboat Association. 020 8776 9890 www.camdencanals.org
- Camley Street Natural Park 020 7261 0447 www.wildlondon.org.uk
- British Waterways 0845 671 5530 www.waterscape.com
- The Puppet Theatre Barge at Little Venice 020 7249 6876 www.puppetbarge.com
- Canal trips by boat to and from Camden Lock to Little Venice: The London Waterbus Company 020 7482 2660 www.londonwaterbus.com
  Jenny Wren 020 7485 4433 www.walkersquay.com
  Jason's Narrowboats 020 7286 3428 www.jasons.co.uk

Books to read
- *Thursday's Child* by Noel Streatfeild. The story of an orphan called Margaret Thursday who runs away to join the navvies on the canal.
- *Angelina, Star of the Show* by Katharine Holabird and Helen Craig

Did you know?
- The poet Robert Browning named this area of London Little Venice, because the canals reminded him of Italy.
- Every time a boat passes through a lock, a lock full of water is lost from the highest point of the canal. The canals therefore need to be filled constantly from the top.
- Nearby Clerkenwell is often called Little Italy, because of the number of Italian immigrants who settled there.

25. The Wild Woods and Dulwich Village

The Adventure

Venture out on the train to one of the ancient woodlands of London, Dulwich and Sydenham Hill Woods. The walk takes you to the woods, through the glories of Dulwich Park, Dulwich Village and the Dulwich Picture Gallery, and back via one of London's oldest toll gates to the station, where you began.

London is a series of villages that have merged into one great amalgam that now makes up the city. Dulwich is one of the oldest and best preserved villages of them all. With much of the land owned by the Foundation of the boys' public school Dulwich College, there has been little modern development and public transport only touches the fringes of this idyllic South London enclave. Consequently, the clapperboard fences, gravelled drives and neat Georgian detached houses have been unchanged for years. The chapel, park, schools and woodland could be miles from a city, but in fact you are only four miles from the West End, ten minutes on the train, something that draws commuters here.

How far? 5.6 km/3½ miles
Start and finish Sydenham Hill station

Walk the Walk

1. Come out of the station and cross the zebra crossing on College Road in front of you to the footpath into the woods ahead. On the left, less than halfway up, is a black gate leading into Dulwich Wood. Turn left here and follow the muddy path between the trees, sticking to the main path up the hill.
2. After a while, you will reach a crossroads of five paths in a wide circle with benches. Go straight across, taking the path that veers slightly to the left. The path meanders gently through the woods, eventually passing a small pond and island of two trees. Follow your nose through the trees as the path widens, keeping the golf course, which has appeared to your left, on your left. To your right is Sydenham Hill Woods Nature Reserve, the closest ancient woodland to central London.
3. The path climbs a little towards a black gate and then widens heading straight down the hill, known as Cox's Walk, to Dulwich Common, the main road at the bottom. To your right is a bridge over a disused railway line, where the train would take passengers to see the exhibitions at the Crystal Palace. After the Palace burnt down in 1936, the line fell into

Bat

TREE LEAVES

Ash

Beech

Horse Chestnut

Lime

Oak

Plane

Silver Birch

Sycamore

Willow

disrepair. Explore the woods further by crossing this footbridge and taking a right through the gate into Sydenham Hill Woods. This is the last remaining tract of the ancient Great North Wood which once stretched all the way from Deptford to Selhurst. King Charles I reputedly often came here to hunt. The woods are full of hornbeam trees, a hardwood that was used, before the days of coal, for making charcoal as fuel for London until the 1780s. There is also a cedar tree that is 150 years old. On the ground are wild garlic, dog violets, bugle, fungi, rare insects and animals like foxes. This is also a national hotspot for the stag beetle (the large black one that flies). Look out, too, for woodpeckers. Try to identify different tree leaves and tree seeds as you explore the woods.

Pick your way through. At the far end is a disused railway tunnel, now home to at least five species of bat and part of the Woodland Bat Roost Project. This part of the woods is glorious in spring and is a destination in itself for small ones. Follow the labyrinth of paths in a circle more or less back to where you started and cross back over the bridge.

4. Turn right down Cox's Walk and turn left on to Dulwich Common, opposite the Grove Tavern pub. Cross the road and walk to the entrance to Dulwich Park at Rosebury Gate. Dulwich Park used to be one of the great farms of Dulwich and the lines of great oaks you can still see in the park mark the original farm boundary.

5. Head left into the park, following the wide pathway. Delve into the middle of the park and explore, pass the children's playground, run around the boating lake or buy an ice-cream in the café. There are fabulous bikes to hire here, including recumbent bikes and children's attachments.

6. Keep left, leaving the park via Carriage Drive and Old College Gate, across the road from the Dulwich Picture Gallery. This was the very first public art gallery to be built in England and is worth a visit. Take the children straight to Gallery XI to see Rembrandt's *A Girl at a Window*.

   To explore Dulwich Village, turn right on College Road at the park gate. This is one of the few areas of London where you feel the sprawl of the city has been kept at bay and you've wandered into a time warp. Much of the land is owned by the Dulwich Estate and the private ownership has limited almost all public transport and preserved the village. The centre of the village is marked by the Crown and Greyhound pub (known locally as the Dog), where Charles Dickens often came to drink. The Village Bookshop beyond the lights is open daily and is highly recommended.

7. Retrace your steps past the Dulwich Picture Gallery and walk up College Road. Admire/covet the grand detached houses and smart white painted fences, crossing Dulwich Common at the lights to pass one of Dulwich's famous public schools, Dulwich College. The school was founded by Edward Alleyn, one of the great actors of Shakespeare's day. A very rich man, he bought the Manor of Dulwich and founded Dulwich College, the College of God's Gift. For an extra unexpected treat, go into Dulwich College main reception (in term time on school days, 9 a.m to 4 p.m.) and ask to see Ernest Shackleton's boat. Tucked away in the school is the original 7m/23ft whaler

Grey Squirrel

Dulwich Picture Gallery

Dulwich Picture Gallery was the first public art gallery built in England. The collection was the creation of two eighteenth-century dandies and art collectors, Noël Desenfans and Sir Francis Bourgeois. When they died, they left the entire collection to Dulwich College with instructions to display the paintings for all to see. They chose Dulwich as a setting because of its smog-free, clear air, not too far from London. Sir John Soane was brought in to design the gallery. The oldest painting in the collection is Piero di Cosimo's *Portrait of a Young Man*, painted around 1500.

that Shackleton and his five companions used on their epic open boat voyage across the Antarctic Ocean in 1916, sailing from Elephant Island to South Georgia. Shackleton was once a pupil at the school, which is why it has ended up here.

8. Climb the gentle hill of College Road, past the school and through the Dulwich tollgate, one of the few remaining (no charge for feet), and back to the station on your right after ten minutes.

Eat me, drink me

There are good cafés in both Dulwich Park and the Picture Gallery. The village has cafés, delis and a pizza place. Or try the Crown and Greyhound pub, 73 Dulwich Village (020 8299 4976 www.thecrownandgreyhound.co.uk).

Useful information

- Dulwich Picture Gallery, closed Mondays, except Bank Holidays. 020 8693 5254 www.dulwichpicturegallery.org.uk
- London Recumbents Bike Hire, Dulwich Park. 020 8299 6636 www.londonrecumbents.com
- Village Bookshop, open seven days a week. 020 8693 2808

- Sydenham Hill Woods and Cox's Walk www.wildlondon.org.uk
- Horniman Museum, an excellent free and family friendly museum, open daily. 020 8699 1872 www.horniman.ac.uk

Books to read

Necropolis by Anthony Horowitz. The opening chapter of this action-packed Power of Five thriller features a terrible car crash in Dulwich Village.

Did you know?

- Phyllis Pearsall, the woman who created the *London A–Z*, lived in Dulwich from 1906.
- Enid Blyton was born on Lordship Lane in East Dulwich.
- The French Impressionist artist Camille Pissarro lived near Dulwich for a couple of years in 1870, escaping with his family from the Franco-Prussian war. Two of his London paintings are in the National Gallery, *Fox Hill, Upper Norwood* and *The Avenue, Sydenham*.

Playtime

London is a giant urban playground if you've got some good games up your sleeve. Here are lots of ideas and suggestions of things to do with friends or when on your own, whether you are exploring on the streets, playing in the park or just waiting at the bus stop. Why not pack some paper, crayons, a piece of chalk, a skipping rope, a tennis ball and a bat where ever you go so you've always got something fun and diverting to do.

Street Games
On the London pavements, play the game of not standing on the cracks between the paving stones or the bears will get you. See how long you can keep going and how fast you can go. Read A.A. Milne's poem 'Lines and Squares' – 'Whenever I walk in a London street, I'm ever so careful to watch my feet.'

Pavement Pictures
- Use chalk to draw a colourful picture in the square of a London paving stone.
- Or look out for interesting coal hole covers on the pavements outside old London houses. Make a picture by laying a piece of paper over the coal hole and rubbing with a wax crayon. Collect as many different ones as you can and put this little bit of history into a scrap book of London things.

Hopscotch
Chalk out a hopscotch board on the pavement and find something to use as a marker. The first player throws the marker on to square number one. Jump over this square and land on every other number on the hopscotch. If there are two squares side by side, put a foot in each box. If only one, hop on to it and land on one leg jumping from two feet to one. On your

way back pick up the marker and hop or jump back to the beginning. Once completed the first player throws the marker on to the next number and so on. If you throw the marker on to the wrong square, you lose your turn. If you stand on a line or put both feet down when you are meant to be hopping, you also lose your turn and you have to repeat the number next time. The winner is the first player to complete the game.

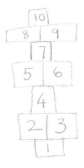

Feet Off London Game

This is a chasing and catch game where someone is nominated 'it' and must catch the other players. If your feet are off London, in other words off the pavement, you cannot be caught.

A Clapping Game

If you are stuck in a queue, waiting for a bus or just plain bored, play this old fashioned clapping game with a friend. Tap your thighs twice and then clap your hands three times. Each time you tap your thighs say these words in this order: Concentration; sixty four; no repeat; or hesitation; you'll go first; and I'll go second; starting with;

At this point you can choose a theme such as nature, countries, cars, films etc. and everyone must take turns to fill the gap on the tap of a thigh. If you repeat something that someone has already said or hesitate before you say your word, the other person wins and you have to start again.

20 Questions

Several people can play this game at one time. Nominate a person to think of something be it 'animal', 'vegetable' or 'mineral'. The rest of the players are allowed to ask 20 questions to discover what it is you have thought of. The person who has chosen the 'thing' can only answer yes or no. If you want to guess the answer before you have used up all the 20 questions you can, but, be aware it counts as a question if you are wrong. The person who guesses the right answer chooses next time.

A variation of this game is 'Who Am I?' where one player thinks of a famous person and the other players have to guess who it is. There is no limit to the number of questions you can ask but the answers can still only be 'yes' or 'no'.

The Alphabet Game

Take it in turns to think up the names of different countries round the world starting with A and working through to Z. When you've got the hang of it pick your own categories such as rivers, sports, plants, animals etc.

A variation on the game is to pick your theme and each person must name something that begins with the last letter of the previous person's word. For example: the first person says Gull, the next person could say Lark, so on and so forth.

One Day I Went to London and I Saw . . .

This is a memory game where you can take it in turns to remember a London landmark. The game starts with someone saying 'One day I went to London and I saw St Paul's Cathedral . . .' The next person would say 'One day I went to London and I saw St Paul's Cathedral and Buckingham Palace . . .' And you go on until the list becomes so long, it is impossible to remember everything you have seen.

Conkers

In the autumn look out for horse chestnut trees and collect as many shiny conkers as you can. Take them home and put your best and biggest ones on strings ready for a conker fight. If your conker breaks your opponent's conker, your conker gains a point and becomes a one-er, a two-er etc. See how many fights your conker can win.

Make a Daisy Chain
Pick daisies in the park in early summer and thread them together to make a headdress or necklace.

Leaf Rubbing
Gather as many different shaped leaves as you can find, take them home and do some leaf rubbings. Lay a sheet of paper over the leaves and rub over with a wax crayon.

Skipping Games
To play Teddy Bear, you will need two 'turners' and one skipper. Jump in and start chanting:
Teddy bear, teddy bear touch the ground (which you do)
Teddy bear, teddy bear turn around (which you do)
Teddy Bear, Teddy Bear say your prayers (which you do)
See how long you can keep up this rhyme before tripping.

To play **chase the Gazelle** you will need two people, one at each end, to turn the rope. You can have as many skippers as you like. Nominate a 'gazelle', who runs through the rope from one end to the other without touching it. Everyone else follows. The second time round each player must jump the rope once. Each subsequent turn, add in a jump until someone is caught by the rope. Keep going. The winner is the player who jumps the most jumps.

Duck, Duck, Goose

You will need a group of friends for this game. Sit in a circle, choose one person to be 'it'. This person walks around the edge of the circle tapping each player gently on the head saying duck or goose. Once you call goose that person must stand up and chase you round the circle. The object is to race after them round the circle before 'it' gets back to and sits down in your place. If 'it' is caught before they get there they have to sit in the middle of the circle until another player takes their place.

Bad Egg

This is a game where a player 'the bad egg' nominates a theme, such as football teams or flowers and the other players must call out one choice from that category. The Bad Egg turns their back to the group of players and throws the ball high in the air and over their shoulder calling out one of the suggestions. All the players must try and run as far away as possible except the players whose choice was called. This person must get the ball as quickly as possible, and then shout STOP! Everyone must stand still with their legs apart and the player with the ball attempts to roll it through one of the other players legs. If successful they pass over the ball to the new 'bad egg'. And if not they become the Bad Egg themselves.

French Cricket

You will need a bat or tennis racquet, a soft ball and two or more players. One player is 'batsman', all the other players are fielders/bowlers. The Batsman stands with his legs together with the bat or racquet in front guarding their legs. The first bowler stands an agreed distance away and throws the tennis ball to the batsman. They hit the ball and one of the fielders picks it up and bowls again from the spot where they picked up the ball. This continues until the batsman gets hit below the knees with the ball, or is caught out.

catching Games

Sevens is a good game to play if you are on your own. All you need is a ball and a wall. Repeat each of the following seven times. You can't progress through the list until you have managed each one seven times without a fault.

- Throw the ball against the wall and catch it without a bounce
- Turn around once before catching the ball
- Clap once before catching the ball
- Let the ball bounce once before catching it
- Throw the ball under your leg and catch it
- Throw the ball under your leg and let it bounce before you catch it
- Throw the ball with one arm behind your back and catch it with one hand
- Make up your own variations

clap and catch is a very simple game to play: throw a ball up into the air and clap once before catching it. On each subsequent throw add in another clap and keep going to see how many times you can clap before you catch the ball.

To play **one Knee, Two Knees** you will need a couple of friends and a ball. Get everyone to stand in a circle. Throw the ball randomly from one to another. When someone drops the ball, there is a list of forfeits to make it all the harder. The first time you drop the ball put one arm behind your back. If you drop it again, stand on one leg, then kneel down, then sit down and finally lie down flat on the ground. If you manage to catch the ball at any point you can get back to standing position by working your way back up the list with each successful catch.

Wild London

Fox

Get some wind in your hair and leave the ancient monuments and tourist hot spots to one side for a day and explore the other London. The city is filled with some of the greatest parks and unspoilt heath. These open spaces, where kings and queens used to hunt, are now the domain of London families and bursting with wildlife and the opportunity for adventure. Get muddy and have some outdoor fun – whether you love cycling, horse riding, swimming, running, rowing, sailing, skateboarding, fishing, bird watching, tree climbing, bat watching or exploring the woods, London has it all. There are canals, lakes, rivers, ancient woodlands, and countless nature reserves.

Wild Woods

There are many small woods in London, the remains of ancient tracts surviving among the houses and roads. But the city is also blessed with great woods, including Highgate Woods in north London, Epping Forest to the east, Dulwich and Sydenham Woods to the south. In late spring head off to see the bluebells and wild daffodils. Pick blackberries, gather conkers and sweet chestnuts in the autumn. Check out the London Wildlife Trust to see what's happening in wild spaces near you. www.wildlondon.org.uk

Fishing

There are lots of opportunities to go fishing in London, on the river, ponds and canals. Here's some useful information to get started:

- You will need a licence if you over twelve years old, and some places require a permit. A National Rod Licence, issued by the Environment Agency, can be obtained from any post office in England and Wales by calling 0870 166 2662, or online at www.environment-agency.gov.uk. Some stretches of river are leased to clubs who can sell you a permit. Visit

British Waterways London, www.waterscape.com, to find your nearest club.

- Thames 21 Tightlines is an innovative angling programme giving young people in London opportunities to learn to fish. For details go to www.thames21.org.uk/tightlines.

Outdoor Swimming

There is nothing like outdoor swimming to get back to nature. London has two places where you can swim wild in natural ponds: the Serpentine in Hyde Park and Highgate Ponds on Hampstead Heath.

- Highgate Ponds, Hampstead Heath. Children must be over eight years old and accompanied by an adult. www.cityoflondon.gov.uk/hampstead
- Serpentine Lido Swimming Club, Hyde Park 020 7706 3422 www.serpentinelido.com

There used to be more than fifty lidos (open air swimming pools) in the city, and a good handful still survive. The best of them are listed below. Most are open in the summer months only.

- Parliament Hill Lido 020 7485 5757 www.cityoflondon.gov.uk/hampstead
- Brockwell Lido, Brixton 020 7274 3088 www.brockwell-lido.com
- Tooting Bec Lido 020 8871 7198 www.wandsworth.gov.uk
- Park Road Lido, Hornsey 020 8341 3567 www.haringey.gov.uk/park_road
- London Fields Lido, Hackney 020 7254 9038 www.hackney.gov.uk
- Hampton Pool, Middlesex 020 8255 1116 www.hamptonpool.co.uk
- Richmond Pools on the Park, Richmond 020 8940 0561 www.springhealth.net
- Oasis Swimming Pool, Covent Garden 020 7831 1804 www.camden.gov.uk/oasis

Horse riding

There are scores of riding schools in and around London. Hack across the open spaces of Richmond Park as Henry VIII and Elizabeth I used to do. Trot through Hyde Park with the Household Cavalry parading past. Canter on Wimbledon Common.
Mudchute Equestrian Centre in the Isle of Dogs www.mudchute.org; Trent Park Equestrian Centre www.trentpark.com; Lee Valley Riding Centre in North East London www.leevalleypark.org.uk; Ealing Riding School in West London, www.ealingridingschool.biz; Hyde Park and Kensington Stables www.hydeparkstables.com; London Equestrian Centre at Mill Hill www.londonridingschool.com; Stag Lodge Stables www.ridinginlondon.com; Wimbledon Village Stables in South West London www.wvstables.com.

On the water

Feel the spray of water on your face on one of London's waterways, a park pond, a canal, reservoir or the River Thames – you can go rowing, sailing or canoeing.
For rowing contact British Rowing who organize rowing courses for eleven years and upwards. To find your nearest club visit: www.britishrowing.org/clubfinder or email info@britishrowing.org. There are various centres for dinghy sailing, such as Surrey Docks Watersports centre www.southwark.gov.uk; Stoke Newington West Reservoir Centre www.gll.org; Westminster Boating Base www.westminsterboatingbase.co.uk; the BTYC Sailsports in Wembley Park www.btycsailsports.org.uk.
For activities on the canals contact www.britishwaterways.co.uk.

Cycling in London

Visit www.tfl.gov.uk/roadusers/cycling/11598.aspx for cycle routes in London and information on cycling proficiency training. You can take a fold-up bicycle on the Underground at any time and other bikes on some lines, off-peak only. Check with Transport for London www.tfl.gov.uk.

London Festivals

January
- The London Parade: every New Year's day follow the floats, marching bands and classic cars as they parade from Parliament Square to Berkeley Square, via Piccadilly. Starts at noon. www.londonparade.co.uk

February/ March
- Chinese New Year: head for the streets of Soho with dancing dragons, firecrackers and crowds of people (don't go with a pushchair). For information go to www.chinatownlondon.org.
- The Great Spitalfields Pancake Day Race: Shrove Tuesday. 020 7375 0441   www.alternativearts.co.uk

March/April
- Easter Monday, London Harness Horse Parade: cart horses of the olden days parade through Battersea Park, a tradition that has been going since 1886. www.lhhp.co.uk

May
- Canalway Cavalcade: narrowboats and Morris dancers at Little Venice. Visit www.waterways.org.uk.

canal boat

- The Covent Garden May Fayre and Puppet Festival: puppeteers perform in the gardens of St Paul's Church in Covent Garden, always on the Sunday closest to 9 May, Punch's birthday. 020 7375 0441   www.alternativearts.co.uk

June
- Trooping the Colour: the Household Cavalry parade for the Queen's official birthday on the second Saturday in June. It has colourful displays, marching bands, Royal Air Force fly-pasts, 41 gun salutes and flag waving. Head for the Mall to watch for free or glimpse the rehearsals on the previous two Saturdays. www.royal.gov.uk

- Last weekend of June. London Dragon Boat Festival: festival in the Docklands, with boat races (morning start) and Chinese food stalls. www.lclc.co.uk

August

- Notting Hill Carnival: the famous street carnival is on the last bank holiday weekend of the summer. The first day is specially set up for children and families. www.thenottinghillcarnival.com

September

- The Great River Race: hundreds of alternative river craft are paddled 22 miles up the Thames from London's Docklands to Ham House in Richmond. See www.greatriverrace.co.uk.
- Thames Festival: a whole weekend festival on the South Bank of the Thames. www.thamesfestival.org

October

- Punch and Judy Festival: Covent Garden based festival of puppet shows. 024 7650 2011 www.thepjf.com

November

- London Children's Film Festival: the Barbican Film Theatre hosts an annual Children's Film Festival to celebrate films for children, with events, workshops and children's filmmaking. www.londonchildrenfilm.org.uk
- Lord Mayor's Show: City of London parade, where the newly appointed Mayor of London is ceremonially processed from the Guildhall to the Law Courts in the Strand and back, accompanied by 150 floats and a firework display into the early evening. www.lordmayorsshow.org

December

- Christmas Tree in Trafalgar Square: Every year since 1947 the Norwegians have given London a Christmas tree to thank Britain for their support during World War II. Over 20 metres high, the tree is put up in early December and decorated in Norwegian-style lights. There is carol singing for all. www.london.gov.uk

HOUSE HUNTING

London has existed on the River Thames in some shape or form since Roman times and successive generations have left their mark by way of buildings. The people of London have lived in everything from Roman villas, through the rickety wooden buildings of medieval and Tudor times, elegant brick Georgian houses and Victorian terraces, to twenty-first-century glass houses. Here is a selection of the sorts of places Londoners live in today.

A typical early Victorian terrace of houses in Chelsea: half London brick (slightly yellow in colour) and half cream stucco. Terraced housing is a good space-saving device for crowded cities.

A pretty coloured canal boat: these floating mobile homes can move according to your whim from the centre of London to the suburbs.

Many old warehouse buildings in the Docklands fell into disrepair but have now been converted into smart riverside homes.

High-rise blocks of flats were a post-war idea to accommodate lots of people on a small area of land. Trellick Tower is notable for its Brutalist architectural design.

Colourfully painted workers' or artisans' cottages provide charming, compact, village-style houses in the city.

Semi-detached villas are typical of smart 'villages' such as Richmond and Dulwich, built while these places were still in the countryside, before London grew to embrace them.

This Edwardian terraced housing built in the early twentieth century is typical of the houses which filled the gaps along roads out of the city between the centre and outlaying villages.

Mews houses are mostly found tucked away behind grand houses in central locations. Once stables for horses, they have become much sought after as homes for chic city dwellers.

These shuttered houses in the East End look just as they did in the eighteenth century when the French Huguenot silk weavers lived and worked in them.

These ships' containers are modern day artisanal live/work spaces. These houses are to be found in a semi-industrial landscape.

INDEX Page numbers in *italic* refer to illustrations.